Louie Bennett

RADICAL IRISH LIVES

Series Editors: Maria Luddy and Fintan Lane

Other titles in the series

Peadar O'Donnell by Donal Ó Drisceoil

Standing L-R: Percy, Lionel, Susan Boulger Bennett, Arthur, Muriel, Susan

Seated L-R: Violet, Claude, James Cavendish Bennett, Louisa (Louie);

Seated at front: Charles Bennett;

(*Reproduced courtesy of Hugh Childres and Diana Stewart*)

THE BENNETT FAMILY

Louie Bennett

Rosemary Cullen Owens

First published in 2001 by
Cork University Press
University College
Cork
Ireland

British Library Cataloguing in Publication Data
A CIP catalogue record for this book is available from the British Library

Library of Congress Cataloguing-in-Publication Data
Owens, Rosemary Cullen
Louie Bennett / Rosemary Cullen Owens.
p. cm. -- (Radical Irish lives ; no. 1)
Includes bibliographical references and index.
ISBN 1-85918-309-3 (pbk. : alk. paper)
1. Bennett, Louie, 1870-1956. 2. Feminists--Ireland--Biography. 3. Women labor leaders--Ireland--Biography. 4. Women--Suffrage--Ireland. 5. Women in the labor movement--Ireland. I. Title. II. Series.

HQ1600.3.Z75 B456 2001
305.42'092--dc21
[B]

2001028987

ISBN 1 85918 309 3

Typeset by Tower Books, Ballincollig, Co. Cork
Printed by ColourBooks Ltd., Dublin

For Simon and David

Contents

Acknowledgements

During the course of my earlier work on the campaign for women's suffrage in Ireland, Louie Bennett emerged as a significant figure meriting a biographical study. Along with other women activists of her generation, Bennett had by and large been overlooked by mainstream historians. I knew that Bennett would not be an easy subject to research as, in contrast with the case of Hanna Sheehy Skeffington, there was no collection of papers readily available. My initial hesitation however, was overcome by the enthusiasm of the Labour Women's National Council, whose members convinced me that this biography *must* be written. My thanks to them for standing by Louie Bennett, and remembering her on all possible occasions. My thanks also to them for the grant they awarded me towards research expenses. Similarly, I wish to express my appreciation to the School of Irish Studies for its support.

My thanks to the staff of the various libraries and archives consulted during the course of this work: The National Library of Ireland, University College Dublin Archives, The National Archives of Ireland, The British Library, The Fawcett Library, London, The British Library of Political and Economic Science, The Irish Labour History Museum. My thanks to Edith Ballantyne of the Women's International League for Peace and Freedom (WILPF), Geneva, for putting me in touch with WILPF archives at Norlin Library, University of Colorado.

This project would not have been complete without the many interviews granted me by former colleagues and relatives of Louie Bennett. Through the varied perspectives of the wide range of people interviewed, it was possible to build a fuller picture of Louie Bennett than existing papers allowed. Many of those interviewed allowed me access to personal correspondence with Bennett. The names of all those interviewed are listed in the notes in this book, but I would like in particular to thank Bennett's niece, Lady Henrietta Wilson, for her continuing encouragement and advice. Similarly, I would like to thank Hugh Childers, Bennett's grandnephew, and his sister Diana.

Among the many good friends and historians to whom I am indebted for their advice are Dr Margaret MacCurtain, Mary Cullen, Dr Maryann Valiulis, Therese Moriarty, Medh Ruane, Hilda and Robert Tweedy, Nell Regan, Joy Rudd, Daisy Swanton, Grainne Blair, the late Andrée Sheehy Skeffington and, above all, Maria Luddy for her constant support and determination that this book *would* be completed!

My thanks to Ailbhe Smyth and the staff of the Women's Education Research and Resource Centre at UCD for their consistent support. Similarly, my thanks to those at the Irish branch of WILPF for all their help. On a personal basis, I wish to acknowledge the practical support and encouragement shown by David Devine, Maura Quinn, Maura Donovan and Anne OLeary.

Last, but not least, my heartfelt thanks to my sons Simon and David. From their childhood through to young adulthood, they have been surrounded by the study and teaching of women's history. This particular book has been many years in gestation. At times, it looked as if it might never be completed. The patience and understanding of my sons at many difficult times during the compilation of this work has been a source of strength to me. I hope they enjoy reading the final product, and I dedicate the work to them as a token of my appreciation.

List of abbreviations

CVO	Commission on Vocational Organisation
DTUC	Dublin Trade Union Council
FUE	Federated Union of Employers
IAW	International Alliance of Women
ICWPP	International Committee of Women for Permanent Peace
IIL	Irishwomen's International League
ILPTUC	Irish Labour Party & Trade Union Congress
INU	Irish Nurses' Union
ITGWU	Irish Transport & General Workers Union
ITUC	Irish Trades Union Congress
ITUCLP	Irish Trade Union Congress & Labour Party
IWFL	Irish Women's Franchise League
IWRL	Irish Women's Reform League
IWSA	International Woman Suffrage Alliance
IWSF	Irish Women's Suffrage Federation
IWSLGA	Irish Women's Suffrage & Local Government Association
IWWU	Irish Women Workers' Union
LPC	Lower Prices Council
NLI	National Library of Ireland, Dublin
WIL	Women's International League
WILPF	Women's International League for Peace and Freedom
WNCA	Women's National Council of Action
WSPU	Women's Social & Political Union

Introduction

Louie Bennett (1870–1956) lived through eighty-six years of global upheaval and transformation. Born in Dublin into a world of nineteenth-century Victorian values, her comfortable middle-class upbringing was not an obvious background for someone who would become active in public life on behalf of women. From the early 1900s, however, Bennett witnessed the radicalization of Irish political life through the emerging labour, nationalist and women's movements. The social and political upheavals affected by these events profoundly influenced her public and private life. Political rights for women, the organization of women workers, pacifism and anti-militarism emerged as key issues that dominated her career.

Initially, it was the campaign for female suffrage which marked her entry into the public arena in 1911. Allied to a growing interest in the labour movement, Bennett extended her work within the suffrage campaign to examine the social and economic position of women workers. During the war years, 1914–1918, Bennett's pacifist convictions were articulated in both domestic and international contexts. From 1917, she became formally involved in the Irish labour movement, becoming General Secretary of the Irish Women Workers' Union – a position she held until 1955. She became the first woman President of the Irish Trade Union Congress in 1932, serving a second term in 1947/48.

Throughout her life, Bennett maintained a keen interest in public affairs at home and abroad. In what might be seen as a forecast of present-day concerns, correspondence during the last years of her life shows her commitment to strengthening links between the Republic and

Northern Ireland, and to the campaign for nuclear disarmament. Bennett's career was not without controversy: she was seen by some as too conservative in her views on equal rights for women, and by others as too middle-class to be a spokeswoman for working women. This biography will examine and evaluate all aspects of Bennett's long and varied career.

1

The early years

Louisa Elizabeth Bennett was born in 1870 into a prosperous Protestant Unionist middle-class Dublin family. Her great-grandfather, William Bennett, belonged to a shipowning family of English merchants. He married an Irish woman, a 'Miss Rowan', and settled in Ireland in the late eighteenth century. Louie's father, James Cavendish Bennett, ran the family business of fine art auctioneers and valuers on Ormond Quay. Her mother – Susan Boulger – came from a family with an army background of some social standing in Dublin. Reflecting the strong class divisions of nineteenth-century society, Susan's marriage to someone 'in trade' was greeted less than enthusiastically by her family. Bennett recorded that her mother's marriage 'was looked upon as a disaster by the Boulgers, who never before had been required to consort on equal terms with "business people"'.[1] The significance of class – and even more particularly of religion – in the new middle-class Dublin suburbs would be clearly outlined by Louie in her reminiscences to R.M. Fox in later life.[2]

Louie was one of nine surviving children – four daughters, Louie, Susan, Muriel and Violet (another daughter died young), and five sons, Charles, Percy, Claud, Lionel and Arthur. Although large by present-day standards, this family size was not unusual for the time. Indeed, within the Bennett family there would appear to have been a tradition of large families. Louie's great-grandfather William had married twice, having a total of eighteen children. Similarly, her grandfather Charles and his wife Elizabeth had thirteen children, and after Elizabeth's death, Charles also remarried.[3]

Louie appears to have had a happy childhood, growing up amid the comforts associated with a privileged background. The family moved house a number of times – from Lansdowne Road to Temple Road in Rathmines and ultimately to Killiney. Details of her early life are sparse and are gleaned principally from interviews in later years. In particular, her memories of the family's years in Temple Road provide a vivid account of middle-class Dublin in the 1880s:

> Temple Road was the refuge of highly respectable business people, anxious to escape from the social zone allotted to the world of trade and commerce. The big, solid houses stand apart from one another, each within its own garden. In my day a sort of hush lay upon the road. Children did not romp there. The voice of the night reveller was never heard. We wore good manners all the time.[4]

Prominent families such as the Gwynns and Dowdens were among her neighbours there. Louie knew neither family intimately at the time, explaining later that they 'were in reality foreigners there'.[5] With regard to the Gwynn family she noted that 'we instinctively realised that they lacked any sense of social barriers. They were misfits on Temple Road'. Significantly Louie recalled that one household was left severely alone:

> The Murphys were not only in business, they were also Roman Catholics. In the 1880s the Catholics were still struggling to penetrate professional circles and were not accepted without question within the fold of Temple Road.[6]

The Murphys were Bennett's next-door neighbours, and it is clear that Louie and her sisters watched with interest the comings and goings of the two Murphy daughters, recalling the touch of glamour they brought to the road with their coachman in uniform, coach and horses. Further interest was focused on the family when the son of new neighbours, who were 'very definitely County', began to court one of the Murphy sisters, and ultimately married her. In her memoirs Louie wondered if 'that refined young lady did not mentally cock a snook at Temple Road when she drove away from it on her wedding morning, leaving it to its impeccable respectability'. Even without the handicap of religious prejudice, that fold of Temple Road was difficult to penetrate and Louie noted that social contacts 'were few and cautious. The wholesale merchant was on a different footing from the retailer. Grocer or auctioneer was ill at ease on Temple Road, but biscuits and furniture held high place.'[7] On a lighter note, she remembered amusing details –

such as Professor Edward Dowden taking his weekly bath in his study in full view of the Bennett family schoolroom, much to the annoyance of Louie's father who warned his children to keep their eyes on their porridge. More irritating to Louie were the rapturous reports of her uncle on the expertise of Professor Dowden's young daughter in performing Beethoven's sonatas and Shakespearean speeches. Louie gritted her teeth during these eulogies, developing 'a profound dislike for Shakespeare, Beethoven and Essie Dowden, as well as a conviction that I didn't want to go to the parties to which Essie did not invite me'.

Although Louie's education began at home, the Bennett family's strong Unionist background determined that Louie be sent to school in England. Her years in England seem to have reinforced her personal non-Unionist stance. Later she would recall:

> I think I was born with an intense hatred of the English people. I cannot help it. I remember that when I used to go along those English country roads and look at those houses, their placidity and comfortability [sic] always affected me.[8]

She appears to have made an impression at her English school, reputedly forming an Irish League, which caused some consternation.[9] Fox states that Louie also attended Alexandra College in Dublin for a time, but she does not appear to have taken any of the formal examinations that were then available to women. She was keenly interested in music and for a time studied voice and music at Bonn in Germany. She had a fine contralto voice and often sang at informal concerts in her youth. Literature, however, was the main focus of Bennett's early years, and her sister Susan recalled how she loved to sit on the floor of her father's library immersed in books. Her biographer, R.M. Fox, likewise observed that Louie 'found refuge in books, for she was always a little reserved and withdrawn'.[10] Among her early favourites were Jane Austen, Charles Dickens, William Thackeray, Samuel Richardson, Henry Fielding and George Meredith. Other literary influences soon emerged. Fox refers to an early essay by Louie in which she identified a parallel between the emergence of an increasingly articulate women's movement and the changing portrayal of women in fiction during the nineteenth century, most significantly in the work of Charlotte Brontë, George Eliot, Olive Schreiner and Henrik Ibsen. Louie credited George Eliot's work with possessing the first hint of women's discontent while she noted that Ibsen's work had given a great impetus to women's progress. However accurate this youthful analysis may have been, these authors profoundly influenced the young Louie who observed that 'the new woman, conscious of untried energies and cramped intellectual powers, shrieked for freedom in her literature'.[11] She described Olive Schreiner's *Story of an African Farm* as 'a cry of rebellion against many things in heaven and earth, but most of all, against the injustice of woman's position in the world'.[12]

Such literature was instrumental in stimulating Bennett to become involved in social and political activities. The Bennett sisters supported late nineteenth-century demands for female suffrage, although none were active in any organization. Other interests absorbed Louie's energies at this time. In the late 1890s she acted as a housekeeper for her brother Lionel while he worked as an engineer on railway construction in Derbyshire and in the north of Ireland. During this period, she and her sister Violet discovered the work of County Antrim novelist Amanda McKittrick Ros. Convinced that Ros's eccentric work of alliteration deserved a wider audience, they sent a copy of her novel *Irene Iddesleigh* to Barry Pain, a London humorous writer and reviewer. His subsequent satirical review of what he termed 'the book of the century' ensured its success, although not quite on the terms that Ros may have desired. In 1898 Louie sent a further Ros novel, *Delina Delaney,* to Pain. In response Pain informed Louie of the virtual cult following which had developed for the works of Ros, recounting how his brother-in-law held 'Delina' dinners at which the book provided the amusement. Bennett and her sisters were invited to attend one such dinner in London.[13] In his later review Pain thanked the Bennett sisters for sending the novels to him. Amanda Ros was furious and wrote in protest to the girls.

There was, however, a more serious side to Louie's correspondence with Pain. A tutor or teacher's notes on an 1891 essay by Louie had advised that she cultivate her writing skills. This essay, titled 'The Melancholy of Modern Poetry', is interesting in that it shows not only the breadth of her reading but also the first indications of a spiritual nature which would become a feature of her correspondence in later years. About 1900, nurturing a desire to be an author, she sought and received Pain's advice on style and writing techniques. Over the next few years she wrote two novels. Prior to the publication of her first novel *The Proving of Priscilla*, by Harpers in 1902 Pain advised Bennett in her dealings with the publishing company as both a woman and a first-time author.[14] Subsequently, her second novel, *A Prisoner of his Word,* was published in Dublin by Maunsel in 1908. The latter title, a quotation from George Meredith (one of her favourite writers), is a romance set at the time of the 1798 rebellion. There were a number of reasons why she chose this topic. Claiming that she always had a great interest in the Irish question, Bennett later related that a friend of hers in Belfast 'induced me to read books relating to the Wolfe Tone and Emmet time'.[15] Another influence is likely to have been the number of events and publications organized to commemorate that rebellion. The novel itself is very much in the genre of a nineteenth-century love story. Through her characters Bennett outlines the ideals which inspired the leaders of the rebellion. Echoing Bennett's own beliefs, the principal male character, Ross Lambart (an Englishman imprisoned for five years for being a member of the United Irishmen) comes to question the wisdom of rebellion, and to believe that 'great reforms are not effected at a blow; only by long and patient striving can a nation grow and gain greatness'.[16] Ultimately however, his love for the heroine – who is committed to armed insurrection – sees him take up arms again, becoming in effect 'a prisoner of his word'. He is saved from the gallows by a melodramatic pardon and a happy ending ensues. Neither book attained the success she had hoped for; R.M. Fox later noted that, 'she had no special gift as a novelist'.[17] It would appear that Bennett resigned herself to this fact with some regret. She never completely gave up on her desire to write, however, and whenever the opportunity arose she contributed to journals and magazines.

Fox presents Bennett as a serious-minded and practical young woman, a strong presence at times of financial crisis within the family, of which there were apparently many. When necessary, she was the one chosen to explain family needs to her grandparents. Her father's death in 1918 and the marriage of most of her siblings left Louie with primary responsibility for her widowed mother and aunt, and later for her invalid brother, Lionel.

It can be argued that the social construct of gender in the first decade of the twentieth century resulted from the work of prominent nineteenth-century pioneers in the women's movement. Irishwomen such as Isabella Tod, Anna Haslam, Anne Jellicoe (all from a Protestant or Nonconformist background), active in campaigns for educational and legal rights for women, provided strong role models for young Protestant women in the early 1900s. Catholic women had few such role models, their role being viewed primarily as within the home or the convent. An interesting comparison can be made between the Bennetts and their near neighbours in Temple Villas, the Giffords.[18] In both of these large Protestant families, it would be the girls who would break away from their traditional background and become involved in contemporary, although different, aspects of Irish public life. In Bennett's case, the example of earlier activists, allied to her wide reading on the women's movement, launched her in 1911 into the revitalized suffrage movement, and into the public arena where she would remain for the rest of her life.

2

Votes for women

During the formative years of Louie Bennett's life the role and status of women in society was being questioned and debated in many countries. The women's movement that emerged prior to 1900 concentrated initially on attaining equal educational rights for girls, legal protection for married women regarding property and children, and a broadening of employment opportunities for single women. Political equality and, more particularly, the parliamentary vote for women, remained an ideal for most activists. While significant developments in the areas of education and property rights were achieved during the 1880s, progress in the political arena was slow. In Ireland, as in England, support for this early phase of the women's movement came primarily from the middle- and upper-class women who could benefit directly from the new provisions. Gradually, such women won the support of male politicians and educationalists in terms of the justice of their demands regarding legal and educational equality. Within the sphere of political equality, accepted mores would prove more resistant to change.

The concept of political democracy based on voting rights was still a relatively new phenomenon. Following vociferous demands, especially by propertied middle-class men, the Reform Acts of 1832, 1867 and 1888 had extended the parliamentary vote to large sections of the population. Nevertheless, the vote remained the exclusive right of propertied males. While initially the parliamentary vote was sought for unmarried and widowed women, a series of Acts between 1870 and 1882, which allowed married women to own property, resulted in political demands by women concentrating on equality with their peers. In effect, the existing property-based suffrage was sought for women. Women's demands for political equality were opposed for a number of reasons. Firstly, despite political and religious differences, the majority of men shared a social outlook which insisted that a woman's place was in the home. Secondly, parliamentary suffrage for women of means was opposed both by those who sought to retain their gender privilege, and by those who sought a more egalitarian adult suffrage. In addition, as women's demands became more vocal and co-ordinated in the early 1900s, political parties came to fear the possible effects of an unknown female electorate.

When John Stuart Mill presented the first petition seeking female suffrage to the House of Commons in 1866 there were twenty-six Irish signatories. One of these was Anna Haslam, a Quaker from Youghal in county Cork, who ten years later formed the first Dublin-based suffrage society.[1] Another pioneer, Isabella Tod, had formed the first Irish suffrage society in Belfast in 1872. Bennett would have been aware of the work of Haslam's group, the Irishwomen's Suffrage and Local Government Association (IWSLGA). In fact, most of the next generation of suffrage campaigners was weaned onto the cause through the work of this pioneering organization. By 1900 women had gained significant advances, notably in the legal and educational fields. Moreover, in 1896 a Bill was passed granting Irish women with certain property qualifications the right to serve as Poor Law guardians. Two years later, the local government vote was granted to Irish women of property. Feminist activists concentrated on encouraging women to support these developments, both by standing as candidates and by voting for women candidates. Like advocates of Home Rule, women would point to their competence in local government as justification for further responsibility. Membership of the IWSLGA increased from this time, with many future prominent militants among the new recruits.

Within a matter of years, however, attempts to curtail these newly won rights alarmed suffragists. In 1903 it was suggested that women be co-opted to Poor Law boards rather than elected, in order to relieve them of the supposed 'worry and turmoil of a popular election'.[2] In fact, closer examination of the 1896 and 1898 provisions show that both Bills merely adjusted the position of Irish women to that already existing for their English counterparts. Extension of these Bills did not imply radical change regarding the status of women in society. Significantly, women were disqualified from serving on county councils and boroughs until 1907 in England and Wales, and until 1911 in Ireland. It seemed that the more power associated with an office, the longer it was withheld from women. Also, despite the gradual admission of women to Poor Law boards and district councils, their role within these boards was often viewed as an extension of their perceived role within the home. Women were seen as carers and their advice was welcomed in the areas of poverty, housing and health, but not in matters of finance and politics. To ensure the retention of these limited political roles, women's groups decided to concentrate on the attainment of the parliamentary vote for women. Existing groups such as the IWSLGA planned to do this through its traditional constitutional methods. However, a significant new element was about to be introduced into the women's campaign – the adoption of militant tactics. The era of the suffragette had arrived.

The emergence of the Women's Social and Political Union (WSPU) in Manchester in 1903, and the militant tactics of its founder Emmeline Pankhurst, marked a significant new phase in the suffrage campaign. Growing awareness of suffrage demands internationally, and the aggressive tactics of the WSPU in particular, inspired many educated young Irish women to become involved in the suffrage campaign. While some initially joined the existing IWSLGA, others took part in WSPU demonstrations and marches, the latter providing what one Irish suffragette called 'a helpful apprenticeship for our campaign in Ireland'.[3] The first in a series of new Irish suffrage societies emerged in 1908 with the formation of the Irish Women's Franchise League (IWFL) by Hanna Sheehy Skeffington and Margaret Cousins. Implicit in its formation was recognition of the quite different political scenario facing suffrage campaigners in Ireland. The IWFL declared itself to be militant, non-party and aimed to obtain votes for women on the same terms as for men. While the extent of Bennett's initial suffrage involvement is not known, she appears on the subscription list of the IWSLGA for 1909 and 1910.[4] The breadth of women's issues and conferences detailed in the annual reports of that association, both within Ireland and abroad, provide a clue as to possible future networking contacts adopted by Bennett.

Over the next few years a number of other suffrage societies were formed, militant and non-militant, catering for particular regional, religious or political groups. Among these were the Munster Women's Franchise League, the Belfast-based Irish Women's Suffrage Society and an Irish branch of the Conservative and Unionist Women's Suffrage Association. Between 1908 and 1912 a campaign of consciousness-raising regarding female suffrage was waged throughout Ireland. Prominent suffrage leaders from England addressed public meetings in Dublin, Cork and Belfast. Corporations, county and district councils were petitioned, and deputations sent to prominent politicians. The pivotal role of the Irish Parliamentary Party in deciding the fate of women's suffrage Bills before Parliament (due to its holding the balance of power) concentrated the attention of English suffragists on Ireland.

It was at this high point of suffrage activity that Bennett entered public life. To co-ordinate the work of the many small societies which had emerged, a federation was proposed. At the inaugural meeting of this body in August 1911, Bennett and Helen Chenevix were appointed joint honorary secretaries of the new organization – the Irish Women's Suffrage Federation (IWSF). It is not clear if the women were friends before this time but it is possible they at least knew of each other through the IWSLGA, to which Chenevix had presented many papers. Chenevix, one of the first women graduates from Trinity College, Dublin, was impressed with Bennett's gift for leadership from that first meeting. She would become a lifelong friend and companion of Bennett, sharing her commitment to a wide range of social issues during the next forty years.

With its head office in Dublin, the IWSF aimed to link together the scattered groups throughout the country, carry out more effective propaganda and educative work and form the basis of an organization which would continue after suffrage was attained. The policy of the IWSF would be non-party and non-militant. Bennett, herself strictly non-militant, refused to condemn any women campaigning for the vote, whatever method they chose. Chenevix later wrote that Bennett had chosen the 'Freedom for Service' motto for the IWSF, asking, 'What is the use of freedom, if it is not the freedom to serve?'[5] As women's organizations were forever under the critical eye of the public, new organizations were particularly anxious to be accepted as serious in their intent. Thus, we find an *Irish Citizen* editorial note in June 1912 apologetically explaining that its earlier reference to the IWSF as a 'loose federation' was not meant to be derogatory, but was intended to describe an association of largely autonomous societies. Between 1911 and 1914 Bennett was engrossed in suffrage activities. Serving as unpaid secretary to the IWSF until 1913 (after which point a paid secretary was employed) she organized meetings, took part in deputations to politicians, kept the press informed of developments and arranged visiting speakers for Irish tours. A 'Friends of Women's Suffrage' scheme was initiated to monitor support throughout the provinces and to help keep country supporters informed of developments.[6] By 1913 fifteen groups were affiliated to the IWSF, rising to twenty-four by 1916. The diversity of groups within the new federation can be judged by its inclusion of members from Unionist backgrounds including authors Edith Somerville and Violet Martin (Somerville and Ross), and nationalists such as Mary MacSwiney. George Russell (AE) was a vice-president from 1915. Although individual members were occasionally involved in militancy. Bennett, while personally non-militant, refused to condemn any woman who used militant methods. Irishwomen from quite disparate backgrounds could now choose between the long-established IWSLGA, the militant IWFL and the middle ground of the IWSF. Activists of the time would probably have agreed with the comment of Margaret Cousins that, 'The era of dumb, self-effacing women was over'.[7]

The long-standing IWSLGA had accepted the formation of the IWFL, despite its militant tactics, as evidence of a resurgence of the women's movement. The formation of the IWSF was greeted more critically by the Association, possibly because it was seen as posing a greater threat to its membership than did an openly militant society. Undeterred, however, the new federation proceeded and member groups increased with the formation of new societies in Belfast and Dublin.[8] Bennett observed that the federation had evolved at an ideal psychological moment. Congratulating its promoters for having gathered together women of different politics and religions, she noted, 'The Irishwomen's Suffrage Federation has had the privilege of affording the outward and visible sign of unity amongst women whom every other influence tended to separate.'[9]

Despite the existence of eighteen suffrage societies within the country at this point, catering for a variety of political and religious backgrounds, there was no distinct nationalist women's suffrage society. Some nationalist women remained outside the suffrage movement, critical of the propriety of Irish women seeking the vote from an alien government, while others who supported the Home Rule cause refrained from suffrage action for fear of jeopardizing the passage of such a Bill. However a number of nationalist women did join existing societies and were able for a time to maintain allegiance to both causes. Events from 1914 would challenge these loyalties.

In many countries, involvement in the suffrage campaign led women into trade union and labour activities. Ireland was no exception. Dublin and Belfast were the two main areas of such co-operation, due to the growing strength of both movements, and to shared ideals of leaders on both sides. The IWFL and the IWSF were the societies most sympathetic to the labour movement, while maintaining their non-party stance. James Connolly wrote at this time that in Ireland 'the women's cause is felt by all labour men and women as their cause . . . the labour cause has no more earnest and whole-hearted supporters than the militant women'.[10] With the exception of Belfast, Ireland lacked a strong female industrial workforce. As a result, membership of Irish suffrage societies from 1908 was primarily middle class. Through involvement in the suffrage campaign many such women became aware for the first time of the problems facing working-class women – issues of housing, sanitation, schooling, health and wages. Helen Chenevix wrote that the suffrage movement 'brought women from sheltered homes face to face with the realities of sweated wages and the wretched conditions imposed on women who had to earn their living'.[11] The formation of the Irish Women's Reform League (IWRL) by Bennett in 1911 is particularly significant in this context. Formed as the Dublin branch of the IWSF, it was the only women's rights society of the time not to contain 'suffrage' or 'franchise' in its title. From its inception it is obvious that a broader platform of women's rights was envisaged than purely the right to vote on the same terms as men. A report by the IWRL in 1912 recorded that:

> The Irish Women's Reform League was formed mainly to establish a Dublin branch of the Irish Women's Suffrage Federation and also to form a working centre for a number of Suffragists in Dublin, who, for various reasons, could not find their right environment with any of the existing societies. It is non-party, it is also non-militant, in the sense that individual members may preach and practice militancy, but the League as an organisation refuses to take militant action.[12]

Meetings were arranged in country districts based on the *Qui Vive* idea whereby small towns and villages were visited and propaganda meetings held in private houses. Bennett conceded that this was a slow and tedious method, but added that the 'personal touch tells enormously, and does much to dissipate prejudice and embitterment. Our people like better to see us in their homes than engaged in the doubtful business of "tub-thumping"!'[13] For work in urban centres, she encouraged open-air meetings of non-militant suffrage societies despite the association of this tactic with the more militant societies. Pointing out the increasing difficulties of getting halls for suffrage meetings, Bennett argued that outdoor meetings were more and more essential as a means of spreading the suffrage gospel. While accepting that 'the ordinary woman finds this distressful', she insisted that 'most Irishwomen have not faced up to the necessity of making sacrifices for the cause'.[14] Bennett used the IWRL to draw attention to the social and economic position of women workers and their families. The IWRL investigated working conditions in Dublin factories, organizing public debates and seminars to discuss its findings. Publication of their findings in the *Irish Citizen* ensured that such information was brought to the attention of a broad spectrum of women's groups. At a four day conference held in December 1913, two days were given over to the topics of women's work in Ireland and women's trade unions. Bennett advised Hanna Sheehy Skeffington that the discussion on trade unions for women should be held in the evening to enable working women to attend.

At this conference, the low wages of Dublin women workers was noted (four to five shillings per week compared to seven-and-a-half shillings in England). Emphasizing the need for women's trade unions, it was pointed out that Dublin had particular problems with large numbers of country girls arriving there prepared to work for a pittance, allied to 'incompetent middle-class girls who worked for little or nothing to earn pocket money'.[15] A series of articles by the IWRL in the *Irish Citizen* investigated specific industrial disputes involving women. In addition to significant discrepancies in wages paid by factories with works in both Dublin and Belfast, health-and-safety issues were highlighted. Among these was the fact that pressure had to be brought to bear on some employers before windows were opened or toilets cleaned. In addition, complaints were made about the use of 'brutal' language towards employees, and in one case, about the preponderance of rats in a chocolate factory.[16] Not surprisingly, high on the list of IWRL demands was the need for women factory inspectors. The League also campaigned for school meals and school medical inspection, advocated technical education for girls and established a committee to monitor legislation affecting women. An IWRL deputation to the Dublin Trades Council led by Bennett in July 1915 reported her interview with the Lord Mayor on the subject of school children's meals. Council members noted that many school managers believed that the provision of school meals was tantamount to socialism. Such connotations were not a problem for Bennett.

A 'Watching the Courts' committee to report on cases involving injustice to women was also established, and the *Irish Citizen* published its findings. Most of the cases reported concerned marital violence, indecent assault on children and the seduction of young girls. Details of such cases were related quite frankly; lenient sentencing, early release of those convicted and judicial attitudes were all challenged and criticized. It was pointed out in one such case (taken against Alderman Kelly of Camden Street in Dublin who was charged with the seduction of two sisters, both servant girls with illegitimate children) that a seduction action could be taken by a girl's father or guardian against her employer for loss of her services.[17] Bearing in mind modern revelations regarding child abuse, it is noteworthy that women activists of this era were aware of and prepared to expose such abuse where possible. Old ideas of propriety remained, however, it being reported that during a divorce case in 1915 the judge requested that 'all ladies' leave the court.

Another initiative of the IWRL was the establishment of a lending library at its Dublin offices, providing books described as 'covering all aspects of the Women's Movement'. Bennett was particularly pleased with this development, arguing that such a valuable asset to the suffrage cause was already 'doing much to rouse interest amongst those who are quicker to respond to an intellectual than to an emotional, philanthropic or moral influence'.[18] Through her key role in the broad range of activities undertaken by the IWRL, we can trace her development from suffragist to trade unionist. Reporting on the work of the IWRL to the *Irish Citizen* in 1913, she advised:

> We have found that our policy of supporting and, where possible, promoting social reforms, has gained us much sympathy. Many people who remain indifferent to the claim of the suffragist for a vote as a measure of justice, are aroused to interest themselves when they are made to see the ultimate objects for which the suffragettes aim – objects which cannot be obtained without the possession of a vote.[19]

In this way, Bennett claimed that the work of the IWRL over the current Insurance Bill· and its involvement in establishing a new vigilance society called the Girls' Protection Crusade, had made many women more fully appreciate the wider suffrage cause. The IWRL co-operated with members of other suffrage societies in patrolling Dublin streets in an effort to protect young girls. A report of one such patrol complained that, 'The whole area of Sackville Street was like one great low saloon, with young girls, soldiers and civilians loitering.'[20] One of the reasons given for young women being on the street late into the night was the number of overcrowded slum dwellings. Announcing that four members of the IWRL (including Bennett) would accept an invitation to serve on the committee of the Citizens Housing League,

M.E. Duggan wrote in the *Irish Citizen*: 'Woman's place is in the home. 20,000 Dublin families exist in "homes" of one room each. Temperance and purity are difficult in such circumstances.' It was pointed out that the Citizens Housing League (which sought the building of working-class housing away from slum areas) included employers and trade union leaders, Catholics and Protestants 'sinking their differences in a patriotic desire to improve Dublin'.[21] Bennett had particular reason to ensure that Catholics were involved in such work. Two years earlier the *Irish Catholic* had criticized the formation of a National Vigilance Association in Dublin, because of its Protestant composition. Promoted by the IWRL, this association had arisen from a meeting in Dublin aimed at the suppression of the white slave traffic. In response Bennett informed the *Irish Catholic* of the involvement of a number of Roman Catholics with the association. She stated further that all Protestants on the present committee were prepared to yield their places to Roman Catholics, and she appealed to more Catholic women to become involved.

When she took her first step into public life through the suffrage movement, Bennett could have had no inkling of the course her life would take. Unfortunately no contemporary account of her thoughts at this time exists. What is clear, however, is the speed with which other related issues soon claimed her attention. With hindsight one can see that the indications of her future commitments were already present in her decision to form firstly a non-militant suffrage federation, followed by a reform league with emphasis on improving the living and working conditions for women. Trade union organization of women, and pacifism interwoven with feminism, were to become the themes that dominated her life. Every task she would take on in subsequent years was approached from one or other – sometimes all – of these beliefs. An IWSF leaflet from this time bears her stamp, admonishing Irishwomen to 'Wake up! Rouse yourselves,' and encouraging women to demand their share in the government of the country 'for the sake of the children and the workers'.[22]

After the general election of 1910 the Irish Parliamentary Party, led by John Redmond, held the balance of power at Westminster, and Home Rule for Ireland seemed a certainty. Parallel to the Home Rule debate was the issue of female suffrage. The gathering momentum of the latter campaign saw a number of attempted women's suffrage Bills introduced in Parliament. While many individual MPs favoured the principle of female suffrage, party consideration usually determined their action if a Bill showed any sign of progressing. With no one party holding a majority, the only prospect for passing a suffrage Bill was through an agreed Bill acceptable to all. With this in mind, a Conciliation Committee drawn from all parties was formed in the spring of 1910 to draft a Bill. Early attempts at such a Bill foundered because of competing priorities. The matter of Home Rule for Ireland – still the dominant issue in Irish and English politics – was a prime cause in hindering the progress of such Bills. Some Irish MPs would have agreed with John Dillon when he declared that women's suffrage 'will, I believe, be the ruin of western civilisation. It will destroy the home, [and] challenge the headship of man, laid down by God.' Other MPs, such as William Redmond (brother of the Irish party leader) and Tom Kettle (married to a sister of Hanna Sheehy Skeffington), actively supported the women's cause in Parliament. However, when Home Rule manoeuvrings demanded, they obeyed the party line. John Redmond – personally hostile to the cause – was most anxious to avoid any issue that might endanger Home Rule, and it was known that Prime Minister Asquith was anti-suffrage.

In 1911 a new conciliation Bill came before Parliament. Intense propaganda was engaged in by English and Irish suffragists to gain support for the measure. The Bill passed its initial reading with a majority vote of 167. Its chances of a successful second reading were undermined by rumours that Unionists would demand a general election if the Bill were passed, thereby posing a threat to the imminent granting of Home Rule. The voting of Irish members was crucial in the defeat of the Conciliation Bill on its second reading in 1912. Whereas in 1911 thirty-one Irish members had voted for the Bill, in 1912 not one voted in favour – not even those who were members of the Conciliation Committee. Fears of endangering Home Rule, either by precipitating a general election or by triggering the resignation of cabinet ministers, were sufficiently strong to convince all Irish members to oppose all women's suffrage measures from that point on. Understandably angry at these developments, suffragists declared war on the Irish Party. When the Home Rule Bill was introduced in the House of Commons in April 1912, it contained no reference to female suffrage, and Irish members were subsequently responsible for the defeat of proposed amendments in this regard.

In England the WSPU bitterly opposed the Home Rule Bill, organising a poster parade outside Parliament proclaiming 'No Votes for Women, No Home Rule'. When John Redmond organized a national convention in Dublin to consider the Bill, women were excluded. A mass meeting of Irish women was held in Dublin in June 1912 to demand the inclusion of female suffrage in the Bill. Suffrage societies from all over Ireland, joined by women trade unionists and nationalists, participated in a mass meeting in the Antient Concert Rooms to support the call for female suffrage in the new Ireland. While the Irish Women's Suffrage Federation and its constituent branches were well represented (Helen Chenevix was on the platform), Louie Bennett was unable to attend, but sent a message of support.[23] A resolution passed at the meeting expressed regret at the proposal to establish a new constitution in Ireland on a purely male franchise, and called on the government to amend the Home Rule Bill by adopting the local government register (which included women). Copies of this resolution were sent to each cabinet minister and to all Irish MPs. It was ignored by all. The IWFL decided to adopt a more militant strategy in Ireland.

Strategies adopted by the various Irish suffrage societies up to this point had followed the ethos of each group. The IWSLGA had continued its long-established routine of public lectures, drawing-room meetings, and appeals to politicians. In addition to regular indoor and outdoor meetings, both the IWFL and the IWSF established branches in London to keep pressure on parliamentarians and to follow developments of interest to Irish women. In January 1912 the IWSF had sent a resolution to all cabinet ministers and Irish MPs requesting that any proposed legislation altering the parliamentary franchise in Ireland should not exclude women. Members of the IWSF joined the IWFL in a deputation to the Chief Secretary for Ireland, Augustine Birrell, regarding the inclusion of women in the Home Rule Bill, and in March 1912 Bennett spent two weeks in London lobbying Irish MPs about the proposed Conciliation Bill. While maintaining close links with English organizations, both groups recognized the need for a perceived separate identity for Irish societies. This was particularly important at a time of heightened nationalist feeling in Ireland. The IWSLGA had suffered in this regard, being dubbed 'an English society' due to its close association with the English National Union of Women's Suffrage Societies, and because of the known pro-Unionist politics of many of its members.

Prior to June 1912, IWFL militancy in Ireland consisted of heckling politicians at public meetings. After that month's mass meeting it was decided to initiate direct militant action on government buildings. This took the form of breaking windows in these offices. The women involved were sentenced and fined according to the amount of damage they had caused. All refused to pay their fines and were imprisoned. Between June 1912 and the outbreak of war in August 1914 there were thirty-five convictions of women in Ireland for suffrage activities. Twenty-two of these incidents took place in Dublin. A total of twelve suffrage prisoners went on hunger strike in Irish prisons, but in contrast to the treatment of suffrage prisoners in England, only two were forcibly fed. Ironically, these were two English WSPU members who had travelled to Dublin to demonstrate against Asquith and Redmond, who were both in the city in July 1912 promoting the Home Rule Bill. When Irish suffragettes were imprisoned, supporters carried out intensive publicity through public meetings and press reports. The prisoners' demand for political status and their adoption of the hunger strike to attain this end earned approval in many quarters. The actions of the English women in Dublin, however, was seen as an attack on Home Rule and caused much ill-feeling against all suffragists for a time. It also caused disagreement among suffrage groups. The IWFL immediately attempted to distance itself from the English protest, publishing a press statement denying any knowledge of the incidents. The IWSF also published a statement disassociating itself from the recent militant action, as did the IWRL. Prior to the Asquith visit, Bennett had been very active on behalf of the IWSF co-ordinating a petition to the Prime Minister which sought equal voting rights for Irish women. She had placed particular emphasis on obtaining postal votes from country supporters. Presenting the petition, Bennett pointed out that it had been signed by some thousands of men and women of all classes and she also highlighted the marked increase in new suffrage societies in Ireland. Bennett argued that when, 'A country is sufficiently awake to demand so clearly and decisively a measure of justice, that demand may not be refused without evil consequences.'[24]

Public outcry in England against forcible feeding of suffragette prisoners led to the introduction in 1913 of a Bill soon to be nicknamed 'The Cat and Mouse Act'. This allowed for the temporary release of hunger-striking prisoners until they were fit to be re-imprisoned. Their period of release would not count as part of their sentence. As re-imprisoned women usually recommenced their hunger strike, under the terms of the Bill sentences could be spread over an indefinite period. This Bill too became law with the support of the Irish Parliamentary Party. Attempts to introduce the measure into Ireland met with widespread protest. The largest protest meeting was held in Dublin's Mansion House in June 1913. Bennett was included on a panel of speakers with Tom Kettle, Dr Kathleen Lynn, Professor Mary Hayden and Constance Markievicz. She seconded a resolution that declared the Act to be 'a dangerous weapon of political oppression', commenting that while she 'personally was an anti-militant, there were moments when non-militants must join with their sisters in protest against some cruelty and injustice'.[25] In the following week she signed a memorial against the Act. Since the first imprisonment of suffrage activists in the summer of 1912, Bennett and the IWRL had written a number of times to the chief secretary's office in Dublin Castle protesting against forcible feeding and also criticizing the Cat and Mouse Act. The increasingly charged atmosphere regarding women's suffrage from 1910 had certainly not diminished Bennett's commitment to the cause. Writing in May 1913 she set out the ideals she would pursue vigorously in the years ahead:

> We are firmly resolved that the Irishwomen's Suffrage Federation shall remain truly and purely an Irish organisation, independent of any similar English association. At the same time we hope that every Irish suffrage society will work to keep alive the consciousness that the woman's movement is a world wide movement; that we suffragists are working for all women; that we recognise the bond of sisterhood uniting women of every nationality without losing anything of the strong, free Celtic spirit and passionate instinct for independence characteristic of that spirit . . . our cause is greater than the cause of a nation, because it is the cause of humanity.[26]

Crucial to the dissemination of information on suffrage activities at home and abroad was the establishment in 1912 of the *Irish Citizen*. This suffrage paper provided feminist activists with an important means of communication, education and propaganda. Its founders – Frank Sheehy Skeffington and James Cousins – were joint editors until Cousins emigrated in 1913. The paper continued to be published weekly under the editorship of Sheehy Skeffington until his murder in 1916. Thereafter, it continued in publication until 1920, with Hanna Sheehy Skeffington and Louie Bennett the main editors during this later period. Designed to cater for both militant and non-militant societies, its columns kept women throughout the country informed of suffrage developments. Articles were published which were expressly designed to educate Irish public opinion regarding feminist demands. Before the launch of the *Irish Citizen*, Irish women had to rely on British suffrage publications. While these did cover the activities of Irish women, inevitably most attention was given to domestic affairs. There had been an earlier Irish women's paper – *Bean na hÉireann* – published between 1909 and 1911 by *Inghinidhe na hÉireann* (Daughters of Erin), a nationalist women's group with a strong feminist bias. Many issues covered by *Bean na hÉireann* were similar to those later covered by the *Irish Citizen.* However, disagreement over whether nationalist or feminist demands should take precedence in the contemporary political scenario, in addition to the strong separatist tone of *Bean na hÉireann,* meant that it appealed only to a section of Irishwomen. Moreover, the *Irish Citizen* made its debut at a peak time of co-operation between women's groups. While its pages reflected a diversity of opinion regarding methods and tactics, they also reflected the vibrancy and commitment of women to their own cause. Divisive political events during the eight years of its publication were inevitably reflected in its pages, but such disagreements only add to its value as *the* most important historical record of the women's movement in Ireland during those years. Bennett was involved with the *Irish Citizen* from its inception, initially as a proof-reader for Frank Sheehy Skeffington, regularly as contributor and, on two occasions, as editor and financial manager. Regular reports on the activities of the IWSF and the IWRL were published. She remained involved with the paper in varying degrees throughout its eight-year existence. In addition to her commitment to the idea of a woman's paper, there can be no doubt that she enjoyed the opportunity to indulge the journalistic ambitions she had never quite managed to quench.

The other key influences on Bennett during these years – the relevance of labour to the women's movement, and the issue of pacifism at home and abroad – emerge in the pages of the *Irish Citizen* during both the Sheehy Skeffington period and in Bennett's own time as editor. Indeed, these two issues along with developments in the nationalist struggle would have a significant effect on the entire women's movement in Ireland from 1913. Although not formally aligned with the labour movement until after 1916, Bennett was moving ever closer to such a direct involvement. She would have agreed wholeheartedly with an *Irish Citizen* editorial in August 1913 which urged women to join trade unions, and called on 'women of the leisured class' to acquaint themselves with the problems of working women. Later that year Bennett forecast that, whether or not Home Rule was established, the Labour Party would become a force in the country. Accepting that the party 'has realised as no other class have done, the need for the economic and political freedom of women', she held back from formal alliance, adhering to the strict non-party suffrage stance. On the question of war and militarism, she and Frank Sheehy Skeffington were of one mind, seeing both as the ultimate threat to feminism.

R.M. Fox claimed that Louie maintained 'anti-national' views until after the Easter Rising. Yet I would argue that Bennett's writings before 1916 are more correctly seen as anti-militarist rather than anti-nationalist. There is no doubt that the execution of the leaders of the 1916 Rising created broader support in favour of Irish independence. Bennett, speaking personally in this regard, commented that 'like many other slow converts [it] aroused a great deal of dormant nationalist feeling in me, just as it did in a vast number of people'.[27] Articles published by Bennett and Sheehy Skeffington regarding war and militarism during 1915 indicate clearly that both sympathized with the desire for Irish independence but disagreed with the use of force to attain it. Bennett's vision of 'nationality' was a broad one, implying freedom for all peoples and nations, large and small. In September 1915 Bennett wrote that the tendency of nationalism to set nations in opposition to each other had been challenged during the nineteenth century by various interactions through the arts and science, but above all by the women's and labour movements. The bonds engendered by the last two, she claimed, had become so strong that they tended to weaken the forces of nationalism:

> Workers of the world united by common aims, struggles and sufferings, are disposed to co-operate in friendliness and goodwill, [but due to the current war] foreign policy was left in the hands of a select few whose interests centred in the aggrandisement of their Empire or Country in capitalistic undertakings.[28]

The outbreak of war in 1914, with its implications for the fate of small nations, and efforts by women internationally to stop the killing and find a peaceful solution, profoundly influenced her. It reinforced her belief in the need for an international perspective. Later she would describe nationality as 'a strong and indestructible human instinct, necessary as an incentive to progress, but liable to create world-wide disturbances if denied free expression or exploited for purposes of aggression'.[29]

With the murder by the British Army of Frank Sheehy Skeffington during the 1916 Rising, Bennett lost a colleague, friend and soul-mate. Following her attendance at the courtmartial of his killer, Captain Bowen-Colthurst, she wrote: 'I went out into the great bleak barrack's space, stupidly wondering if I was in the real world. Was it possible that in our city of Dublin, with all its homely associations, all these cruelties had been enacted, all these agonies suffered?' She took some solace in the hope that his death 'would kindle a blaze whose influences none of us here today can measure. For his story ringing through the length and breadth of Ireland, and much further afield, was doing more to weaken the prestige of the militarist system than years of propaganda could do'.[30] She wrote to Frank's widow, Hanna, offering assistance with the *Irish Citizen*. She clearly felt that the work of the paper should not be forced on her at this time, and offered to meet Hanna before she left for the United States to discuss how she could lighten the burden. She did, however, express some misgivings as to the wisdom of continuing the paper under the existing conditions, confessing that she felt no inclination to press for suffrage from the incumbent British government. Despite her misgivings, she became very involved in the production of the paper, and later in 1916 took over its editorship while Hanna was in the US. She helped to organize an *Irish Citizen* fund in memory of Frank, and also suggested that Hanna consider compiling a selection of her late husband's writings for publication. Such a compilation dealing with Irish conditions from the time of the 1913 Lockout would, she believed, form a fine survey of that period, and she felt would make some money for Hanna. Accepting that 'it seems hard to suggest this when you are so tired', she nevertheless felt the project worth doing and offered her help in its preparation.[31] There were times, however, when she was unable to help Hanna, as was indicated by her apology for not contributing a requested article on the English suffrage movement. She explained: 'I hate to refuse you, but I'm simply unable to write what you ask. I could not write on the English suffrage movement in any strain but a diatribe against a servile sex'.[32]

An interesting opinion of Bennett occurs in correspondence to Hanna Sheehy Skeffington from Deborah Webb – a friend of Hanna's and a long-time supporter of the suffrage cause. Commenting on her increasing involvement with the *Irish Citizen*, Webb wrote that 'Louie has written to me twice in a business like and thoughtful manner, and I look forward to getting my copies of the I.C. I have a great admiration for *her* [sic], though I have never met her.' Some weeks later, having met Bennett, Webb confided to Hanna that, 'She is indeed pleasing, staunch and able.'[33] Bennett's other interests and commitments emerge in her letters to Sheehy Skeffington. We find her asking for a copy of Padraig Pearse's *Ghosts* and *The Sovereign People*, the latter she desired 'very particularly'. The importance of family commitments is also apparent in her correspondence. Her father was very ill towards the end of 1916 and she had to curtail her meetings, explaining to Hanna that her mother 'cannot get out unless I am home'. As the only unmarried daughter, Bennett was to fill the traditional role of carer for her parents and an unmarried brother, juggling such responsibilities with an ever-expanding career.

When Hanna Sheehy Skeffington resumed her editorship of the *Irish Citizen* on her return from the United States in the late summer of 1917, Bennett continued as a regular contributor. Allied to her continued activity with the IWRL, and with the pacifist campaign at home and abroad, increasingly her contributions from 1916 reflected her growing links with trade unionism (Bennett's career with the Irish Women Workers' Union will be examined in Chapter 4). In October 1917, expressing views similar to those of James Connolly, she wrote: 'The rapid development of organisation in the Irishwomen's world of labour is the best possible contribution to the whole cause of feminism. There can be no real freedom and independence for women until they are economically free.'[34] By 1920, the *Irish Citizen* was devoting a special page to women workers 'in accordance with the policy of feminism, peace and labour for which it had always stood'.[35] In March that year Bennett took over editorial and financial responsibility for the paper. That there was some disquiet at this development can be gauged from her comments to Emily Balch (International Secretary, WILPF) of her intention to run the paper primarily as a journal for women workers, 'but Mrs. Skeffington is unwilling to give me full control, and we don't see eye to eye on labour questions'.[36] Bennett was personally optimistic, however, regarding the success of the venture, advising Hanna Sheehy Skeffington to 'pull me up whenever you like . . . I do not fear serious disagreements with you'.[37] But disagreements there were, ranging from the issue of tobacco advertising in the paper to the acceptability of a 'home hints' column.

To offset increasing unemployment among Dublin women tobacco workers caused by imports from England, Bennett planned an advertising campaign for the *Irish Citizen* encouraging Irish people to smoke only Irish tobacco. She hoped that this would not be contrary to her editor's principles. When she discovered that Sheehy Skeffington did not, in fact, approve she conceded that only a passing reference to the British tobacco combine would be made. She jokingly apologized to Sheehy Skeffington for her moral sense being so sadly deficient. Bennett also informed Sheehy Skeffington of her intention to initiate a series of articles on what she called 'The Mistress and the Maid problem'. Commenting that constructive thought on the subject of the home and the modern woman's place therein would be valuable, she noted the 'need to clear our minds a bit on the subject'.[38]

Bennett's introduction of a 'home hints' column (aimed at women in the home) caused further disagreement and much heated debate. Kathleen Connery of the IWFL scathingly attacked what she termed 'this kind of literary dish wash'. She believed that the *Irish Citizen* should teach women self-respect and self-reliance beyond the four walls of the living room. In reply Bennett asked, 'Is not housekeeping woman's primary duty, and should not the art of doing so be a prominent feature in any woman's journal?' The controversy raged through a few issues with correspondence to the paper showing strong feelings on both sides. Bennett defended the inclusion of such articles by comparing the life of women in the home with that of men in the shop or factory – the latter she described as 'very dull and full of drudgery' while 'housekeeping needs to be organised, [and] better methods employed'. Many feminists believed that such a column indicated a regressive attitude to women's progress. Interestingly, most of those who agreed with Bennett were single while most who disagreed were married, indicating perhaps an idealized image of life in the home by those who were not confined there. Bennett was unapologetic, commenting that the '*Irish Citizen* need lose none of its spiritedness if it deals with this subject and endeavours to raise it to a higher status in woman's mind'.[39] The issue of domesticity would be raised on a number of occasions by Bennett during her career. During the war years of 1914–18 she had pointed out in the *Irish Citizen* that women had been excluded from any position requiring initiative or intelligence. Criticizing male retrenchment committees which lectured women on how to economize in their housekeeping, she commented: 'we ought to rebel when we see men taking over the tasks which are specifically women's work'.[40]

While Louie Bennett's position as secretary of the IWWU placed her in a key position to demand equality of opportunity for women in all areas of work, her *Irish Citizen* articles solidly reflected acceptance of the prevailing conservative attitude towards women and home. Late in 1919 she initiated a debate in the *Irish Citizen* on the need for a separate women workers' union. Arguing in favour of this she insisted that, given current societal and economic realities, the time had not come for women to break in on men's industrial preserves.[41] Another main area of disagreement between Bennett and Sheehy Skeffington was the changing ethos of the paper from being a feminist suffrage paper to a feminist trade union paper. From 1918, more and more space was given to women workers' news, union activities and pay disputes. In January that year, describing the growth of women's trade unionism as the most important development in the Irish woman's movement in the past year, Bennett suggested that the paper formulate a definite policy in accordance with the new ideas of the day. She asked if the *Irish Citizen* would become the organ of economic justice for women. In reply, Sheehy Skeffington argued that the paper had always been that and would be happy to continue publishing details of such work. And indeed the paper continued to so do. In 1914, when incorrectly quoted as favouring union with the Labour Party, Bennett had stated that she considered it inadvisable to form a union with any party. While firm allies would be found within Labour, she argued that 'suffragists and labourists might do mutual services for each other whilst remaining absolutely independent.'[42] In similar vein, an editorial by Hanna late in 1919 emphasized the continued need for a distinctly non-party feminist paper, 'Our editorial policy must remain feminist and non-party [as] no party, unhappily, is yet quite free from sin where women are concerned.'[43]

Despite this clear non-party stance, the first issue of the *Irish Citizen* published under Bennett's management in spring 1920 announced the decision of the IWWU and the Irish Nurses' Organisation to use the paper as their official journal. Tensions consequently increased between Bennett and Hanna Sheehy Skeffington, with Bennett pointing out in July 1920 that she must cater for her audience and that changes would have to be made if sales were to increase. Accepting that many old readers might object to 'our particular line of stuff', she hoped to make the paper popular among working-class women. She made it quite clear that as long as she took financial responsibility for the paper she would persist along her own lines. Shortly afterwards she told Sheehy Skeffington that she would like to take over the paper completely and develop it as a feminist labour paper. This proved to be the last straw for Hanna who cancelled their agreement. Bennett appears to have been surprised at this. Her correspondence with Sheehy Skeffington certainly shows that she was sorry for the way that things developed and that she hoped 'to start a little paper of our own to cater for our own people'.[44] Unfortunately, unease with IWWU dominance within the *Irish Citizen* did not always rest on feminist principles. When news broke of the cancelled agreement, one suffragist wrote to Sheehy Skeffington hoping that the paper would continue under her direction commenting that, 'We want moral and temperance points raised, not anti-[Liberty] hall squabbles . . . I fear women workers are likely to be no use re morality and temperance.'[45]

For a variety of reasons, the *Irish Citizen* was nearing the end of its publishing life. The Representation of the People Act of 1918 had seen the partial attainment of suffrage objectives. By granting the parliamentary vote to women of thirty years of age and over, while simultaneously extending the vote to men of twenty-one years, this Act avoided the immediate establishment of a female majority in the electorate. Around the world many feminist and socialist groups had disintegrated under the impact of war. Where suffrage groups survived they faded away once the vote was granted, their *raison d'être* removed. The tenuous coalition of women of differing political views was no longer necessary and women's solidarity split on party lines. While most Irish suffrage societies remained intact during and after the war, increasingly the energies of suffragists were drawn into the political struggles of the day. In what would be the final issue of the *Irish Citizen* late in 1920, Sheehy Skeffington summarized the pressures currently facing Irish women. In particular, she noted that the ongoing separatist, armed struggle had impelled the woman's movement into temporarily merging with the national movement. She referred to the recent choice offered to the paper of becoming the organ of an admittedly important section of women workers, and of attempts to include in the paper a 'home chat' section. The former was refused because it was felt that the paper should be the organ of all women, not just a section, and the latter because it was felt inappropriate for the *Irish Citizen* which had 'other interests to serve'. Significantly – and sadly – she noted: 'There can be no woman's paper without a woman's movement, without earnest and serious-minded women readers and thinkers – and these in Ireland have dwindled perceptibly of late.'[46] Sheehy Skeffington's observations were confirmed over the coming decade when political differences hindered the continuation of a cohesive women's movement. Many of the women who entered the political arena post-1916 did so from a nationalist, not a feminist, perspective. Political division among women, allied to the absence of a strong unified women's forum, would be particularly noticeable during the 1920s, when a series of government measures restricting women's rights were introduced. Pioneers from the suffrage campaign did, however, become active in specific areas, most noticeably in the pacifist and trade union movement. In both of these areas Louie Bennett would be a key figure.

3

Pacifism, militarism and republicanism

The outbreak of war in 1914 had serious repercussions for the women's suffrage movement worldwide. That movement had become increasingly international in outlook from 1904 with the formation of the International Woman Suffrage Alliance (IWSA) by women from the United States, Australia and Europe.[1] This group is still in existence under its later name of the International Alliance of Women. Among its first elected officers were Susan B. Anthony and Carrie Chapman Catt, both Americans; Dr Anita Augsburg from Germany and Mrs Millicent Garrett Fawcett from Great Britain. Described by Richard Evans as representing the dynamic side of feminism, the IWSA voiced radical feminism on an international level, giving members a sense of belonging to a great and irresistible current of world opinion.[2]

During the first ten years of the IWSA, a series of international congresses was held, with ever increasing representation from member countries. Irish activists were kept informed of developments through the suffrage press. In 1913 the seventh and largest such conference was held in Budapest. Among the 300 official delegates from twenty-two countries, were three Irishwomen – Hanna Sheehy Skeffington from the IWFL, Louie Bennett from the IWSF and Lady Margaret Dockrell from the IWSLGA. This meeting of prominent and committed women activists reads like a 'who's who' of the early women's movement.[3] Charlotte Despard's biographer has noted that the 'international stance of so many suffragists during the First World War owed something to the contacts made at Budapest'.[4] Within a year, however, political developments placed the unity of the IWSA under severe strain. When war broke out in August 1914, Louie Bennett was in the US visiting her brother Claud. She returned home immediately and from this point on became a leading pacifist voice in Ireland. In fact, from the beginning of the war a significant section of the international suffrage movement adopted a pacifist stance, thus causing division within most national women's organizations. For example, in the same month that nationalist German women cancelled the 1915 IWSA congress planned for Berlin, anti-war German suffragists published an open letter extending their hand 'to our sister-women . . . above the war of the nations'.[5] In Ireland the IWSF welcomed this statement, rejoicing that the bond of universal sisterhood had risen above the present fierce struggle and thereby providing a hopeful voice for the future. Bennett was among one hundred 'British' signatories to a Christmas letter to the women of Germany and Austria published in *Jus Suffragii* (Journal of the IWSA) in January 1915.[6]

Following an American tour by feminist campaigners Rosika Schwimmer (Hungary) and Emmeline Pethwick-Lawrence (Great Britain), a Women's Peace Party was formed in the United States in January 1915 by Carrie Chapman Catt (President of the IWSA) and Jane Addams.[7] These developments were followed with close interest in Ireland. Unlike many suffrage organizations worldwide, the three Irish associations which had been represented at Budapest continued throughout and after the war of 1914–18. This was a testament to the commitment of such groups to the cause of suffrage rather than a reflection of a unified stance regarding the war. In fact, there was a wide variety of opinions as to the correct stance for women in Ireland at this time, particularly in the early war period. Generally speaking, societies with close English connections abandoned or postponed all suffrage work and became involved in war relief works. The IWSLGA was most involved in such works, which ranged from the making of bandages for veterinary hospitals in France to the endowment of a hospital bed in Dublin Castle Red Cross Hospital for wounded soldiers. Jingoistic references in their annual reports to 'our brave soldiers and sailors' and to the fact that 'women are helping to save our empire' offended nationalist women and feminists who considered such activities inconsistent with the aims of suffrage societies. The IWSF and the IWRL also became embroiled in controversy. An emergency executive meeting of the IWSF in August 1914 proposed the suspension of active suffrage propaganda and the organization of constructive relief work. Accordingly it was decided to support the newly formed Emergency Council of Suffragists, which aimed to provide a forum wherein suffragists could engage in remedial work without abandoning suffrage ambitions. Projects included the establishment of workshops in Dublin employing 100 girls.[8] The IWRL was particularly committed to involving women in temperance work and to the protection of young girls on the streets. Statistics were compiled on intemperance in Dublin and the League was responsible for the temporary closure by the military of 'two obnoxious public houses'. The IWRL also opened a café and recreation centre for women, and voiced its concern at the opening of a munitions factory in Dublin. It demanded minimum wages for the women employees and the appointment of at least one woman on the munitions tribunal.

The *Irish Citizen* had made its anti-war stance clear from the beginning of the war, causing offence to groups such as the IWSLGA. Publication of its poster 'Votes for Women Now! Damn your War' was also objected to by some members of the IWRF, not from pro-war convictions, but because such condemnation was seen as outside the remit of a non-party suffrage organ. Some criticism rested also on the use of the word 'damn'. In response to members' disapproval, the IWRL ceased to sell or subscribe to the *Irish Citizen* – a policy that continued for three months. Further controversy ensued within the IWSF when its Cork branch – the Munster Women's Franchise League (MWFL) – presented an ambulance to the military authorities. This action forced the resignation of Mary MacSwiney, who declared that the majority of members were 'Britons first, suffragists second, and Irishwomen perhaps a bad third'.[9] Bennett wrote to Sheehy Skeffington at this time expressing her feeling of despair that women's groups were 'like sheep astray and I suppose when the necessity of knitting socks is over – the order will be – Bear sons, and those of us who can't will feel we had better get out of the way as quickly as we can'.[10] Early in 1915 the IWSF reversed its policy regarding the suspension of suffrage activities. Pointing out that its objective was the enfranchisement of Irish women and that all philanthropic activities were of secondary importance, it urged members to work for attainment of this objective before the end of the war. Louie Bennett would have been influential in this decision, writing in the *Irish Citizen* that, 'Women should never have abandoned their struggle for justice, war or no war.'[11] Asked by Sheehy Skeffington to write a piece on women's wartime work, Louie replied disconsolately: 'I'm afraid I would have nothing to say about occupations open to women through the war, whatever I might have to say about occupations closed.' She did later write such an article for the *Irish Citizen*, commenting:

> Since the war began, with one notable exception, I do not think any position demanding the use of brains has been entrusted to a woman. Women have been asked to knit, to nurse, to collect tickets, to deliver letters, to make munitions, to do clerical work of every kind, but from any work in which they could utilise their intellectual gifts or show any powers of initiative, they have been and are rigorously excluded. Women ought to protest and rebel against this criminally stupid disregard of a rich fund of intellectual energy. There is no patriotism in passive submission to such blundering dominance.

Referring to trade union fears of problems to be faced at the end of the war regarding the low pay of women workers who had taken men's jobs, she declared:

> At a moment when it was futile to demand enfranchisement [women's suffrage societies] could have maintained the demand for 'equal pay for equal work', and the struggle to raise the social status of woman so that she might not be treated as a pawn in a game.[12]

In September 1914 the Hungarian feminist leader, Rosika Schwimmer, travelled to the US to present President Wilson with a plan for a conference of neutral nations. Soon after the formation of the Women's Peace Party in the US early in 1915, the IWRL suggested to the IWSF executive that a campaign be initiated to educate public opinion against the prevailing militarist spirit. Louie Bennett – the proposer of that motion – asked in *Jus Suffragii*:

> Are we right to tolerate in silence this modern warfare, with all its cruelty and waste? More and more the conviction grows that it is full time that women rose up and demanded with no uncertain voice a truce for reflection, for debate upon the questions.

While acknowledging that many deeds of heroism had helped people keep faith, she cautioned:

> Let us not blind ourselves with talk of the glories and heroisms of war. We dare not ignore the moral and spiritual wreckages that remain unchronicled. We have to think of men brutalised and driven to hideous deeds by their experiences; of men with reason destroyed and nerves shattered; of men disgraced for lack of the cold courage that can face the horrors; of men with faith in good slain, their outlook on life eternally

> embittered. Nor do such losses fall upon men only. What of the women for whom the French Government has to devise legislation to deter them from infanticide? What of the children begotten under such conditions?

Appealing to the 'Women of Europe' to create the will for peace, Bennett noted:

> Each woman in her own place can begin that work now. She can dedicate herself to the cause of peace, pray for it, *think* for it, influence others to join with her in a league whose motive force shall be the will for peace. A nucleus of women here, there, everywhere, thinking and working thus, will eventually permeate the public mind with their desire.[13]

In the *Irish Citizen* she urged all suffrage societies to organize meetings and study groups on the issue. The IWFL strongly supported these developments. Weekly articles and editorials in the *Irish Citizen* kept women informed of progress.

Following the German withdrawal from the invitation to host the 1915 congress, the IWSA president, Carrie Chapman Catt, cancelled the conference entirely. Many members vigorously disagreed with this decision. In response, a group of Dutch suffragists organized a meeting with women from Belgium, Britain and Germany in Amsterdam in February 1915. From this emerged a plan for an international women's peace conference in the Hague on 28 April 1915.[14] The *Irish Citizen* monitored these developments in Ireland. However, at a conference held to discuss possible Irish participation, fears were expressed by some that such activity might imply disloyalty to those fighting at the front. Recording 'hot debates on the Peace Congress Scheme' at committee meetings of the IWRL, Lucy Kingston concluded that Ireland would not be represented 'simply because of ultra Loyalists' objections'.[15] Similar sentiments were being expressed throughout Europe. In the British press, intending participants were derided as 'pro-Hun peacettes' going to 'pow-wow with the fraus', and their desire for a negotiated peace was denounced as treachery.[16] Almost all governments tried to prevent their women attending the Hague conference. German delegates were stopped at the Dutch border, but twenty-eight managed to get through. No French or Russian woman was able to attend. The American delegation of forty-one was delayed on government orders in the British channel for three days and delegates arrived just after the Congress started. From a total of 180 British delegates only twenty four were, very reluctantly, granted travel permits by the Home Secretary, an action almost immediately negated by the announcement that all cross-Channel travel was suspended indefinitely. Only three British women actually reached the Hague – two had crossed some days earlier, and the other had travelled with the United States contingent.

While feminist groups in belligerent countries adopted varying degrees of nationalist rhetoric, the situation of Ireland posed particular difficulties. Initial differences within Irish suffrage societies reflected pro- and anti-war positions, on either loyalist or feminist grounds. Despite these divisions, some Irishwomen planned to attend the Hague conference, and an Irish committee was formed from the various suffrage societies to promote the event. It was decided to send seven delegates.[17] Of these, only Louie Bennett was granted a travel permit, and in the event was prevented from travelling due to the Admiralty embargo. A public protest meeting was called in Dublin on 11 May by the IWFL to protest against the government's action. James Connolly and Thomas MacDonagh were among the speakers. In a letter of support, Patrick Pearse declared the incident another example of British policy to exclude Ireland from international debate, adding that much good would be done if the incident ranged more of the women definitely with the national forces. Echoing unease with nationalist attitudes towards suffragists, Margaret Connery of the IWFL, chairing the meeting, asked why it would not range more of the national forces definitely with the women.

Particularly significant for Irish pacifists was the development of strong nationalist and separatist feeling, and a desire to make England's difficulty Ireland's opportunity. In an environment where both nationalists and loyalists prepared for military confrontation, pacifism became an increasingly unpopular notion. This reflected worldwide reaction to feminist peace campaigners during the war years, with the overwhelming majority of women's groups in all countries supporting the war effort.[18] Louie Bennett and Frank Sheehy Skeffington were among the leading Irish proponents of pacifism during this period. From the outbreak of war the latter had continuously published anti-war articles in the *Irish Citizen.* Arguing that war was one of the social evils arising from the subordination of women he declared that:

> War is necessarily bound up with the destruction of feminism . . . feminism is necessarily bound up with the abolition of war. If we want to stop wars, we must begin by stopping this war.[19]

Bennett, echoing current debate on feminism and militarism, wrote in the *Irish Citizen*:

> Suffragists of every country must face the fact that militarism is now the most dangerous foe of woman's suffrage, and of all that woman's suffrage stands for. The campaign for enfranchisement involves now a campaign against militarism. And if we are to conquer militarism we cannot postpone doing so for any 'whens' or 'untils'.[20]

Debate during and after the Dublin protest meeting regarding the Hague conference shows that these issues were now clearly set in an Irish context. Thomas MacDonagh's address to this meeting laid bare the thorny dilemma with which Irish suffragists would have to grapple within the year. Declaring openly that, as one of the founders of the Irish Volunteers, he had taught men to kill other men, and had helped to arm thousands of Irishmen, he nonetheless described himself an advocate of peace 'because everyone was being exploited by the dominant militarism'. Acknowledging his anomalous position, his one apology for helping to articulate a different kind of militarism in Ireland was his belief that 'it would never be used against fellow countrymen'.[21] Bennett voiced her concern at the tone of this meeting in the *Irish Citizen*:

> Militarism in the most subtly dangerous form has its hold upon Ireland. Those women who take up the crusade against militarism must not tolerate the 'fight for freedom' and 'defence of rights' excuses for militarism. To use barbarous methods for attainment even of such an ideal as freedom is but to impose a different form of bondage upon a nation.

Stating her considerable dissatisfaction with the ideal of pacifism reflected by the meeting, and disappointment at the obvious lack of any sense of internationalism as a world force, she argued:

> If [Ireland's] nationalism is real and vital, it will suffer no loss from a generous attitude of mind towards the country to which she is for the moment subject. The nation which cherishes wrongs and old hatreds becomes bound up spiritually as well as politically.

Bennett hoped to see Irishwomen rising to the task of developing such a spirit of internationalism, pointing out however that:

> They cannot do so unless like those Belgian, German, and Englishwomen who attended the Hague Congress, they are willing to surrender certain national prejudices and inherited enmities.[22]

Writing privately to Hanna Sheehy Skeffington, Bennett noted that the tone of the meeting was far more anti-English than anti-militarist, and that while the present war was reckoned barbarous and immoral, it would appear that a war for Ireland would find many supporters.

> That seems to me a thoroughly superficial form of pacifism – hardly worthy of the name. I do not care for a pacifism which is not truly international, which is not tolerant towards *all* nations. I shall in future take no part in peace meetings which put Irish nationalism above international tolerance, and which are embittered by anti-English feuds.[23]

This was not the first time she had expressed concern at anti-English or pro-war sentiments. Responding to a request from Hanna Sheehy Skeffington to speak at a suffrage meeting early in 1915, Bennett asked:

> Can you arrange that all controversial topics in connection with the war – such as pro-Germanism, recruiting etc., be ruled out of order. I am strongly of the opinion that our personal bias on these questions should be, as far as possible, submerged when we come together as suffragists.[24]

Similarly, when Hanna sought her help with the *Irish Citizen* in June 1915, Bennett agreed, but stated:

> I will gladly do what I can with Citizen – but I must protest against such fiercely anti-English articles as that signed M.B.D. in this week's issue. It is surely inadvisable to allow a suffrage paper to become a partisan paper – and still more inadvisable to run the risk of having it suppressed.[25]

While Louie and Hanna would ultimately differ on the issue of justifiable warfare, the following extract from Hanna's letter to Thomas Haslam early in 1915 shows her still close to Louie's viewpoint:

> Mr. Haslam must remember that every war is regarded by each country engaged in it as a sacred and holy war. It is always the other side that is the aggressor. We are always fighting for religion and freedom; the enemy (the ally of yesterday, the friend of tomorrow) is always the foul foe of civilisation and progress. Women must rid their minds of such cant by cultivating a necessary detachment which will regard war in itself as a crime and a horror unspeakable.[26]

The debate was widened by the publication of an *Open Letter to Thomas MacDonagh* by Frank Sheehy Skeffington in response to the public protest meeting. In this Skeffington enunciated clearly the views of pacifist feminism towards militarism, and in particular towards Irish militarism. Commenting on MacDonagh's speech, Skeffington noted:

> You spoke vehemently and with unmistakable sincerity in advocacy of peace. You traced war, with perfect accuracy, to its roots in exploitation. You commended every effort made by the women to combat militarism and establish a permanent peace. And in the same speech you boasted of being one of the creators of a new militarism in Ireland; High ideals undoubtedly animate you. But has not nearly every militarist system started with the same high ideals?

Skeffington considered it highly significant that women were excluded from the organization, indicating a reactionary element in the volunteer movement. While agreeing with the fundamental objectives of the Irish Volunteers, and acknowledging its merits, Skeffington commented:

> As your infant movement grows, towards the stature of a full-grown militarism, its essence – preparation to kill – grows more repellent to me . . . European militarism has drenched Europe in blood; Irish militarism may only crimson the fields of Ireland. For us that would be disaster enough.[27]

Shortly before the Easter Rising, Louie Bennett and Frank Sheehy Skeffington took part in a public debate with Constance Markievicz on the motion, 'Do We Want Peace Now?' Of the five or six hundred attending, only a handful supported Skeffington. Bennett was appalled that Markievicz and her supporters preferred to see the war continue if it meant defeat for England and subsequent freedom for Ireland. She intervened, strongly disagreeing with what she saw as cowardice. James Connolly spoke after her, promoting the idea that now was the time to strike against England. Bennett later wrote that this meeting had depressed her, describing its spirit as 'bad, sinister, lacking in any idealism to redeem its bitterness'.[28] Some months earlier Connolly had interrupted a Dublin meeting of the Union of Democratic Control (UDC) addressed by Helena Swanwick, pouring scorn on her argument that Britain stood for the rights of small nations.[29] While admiring Connolly intellectually and praising him as a thorough feminist, his commitment to military action prevented Bennett from working with him in the labour movement (see Chapter 4). In the last issue of the *Irish Citizen* edited before his death, Frank Sheehy Skeffington warned Irish pacifists that the military authorities were planning a pogrom of those opposed to them that would provoke resistance and lead to bloodshed. Bennett too was alarmed at the pace of events. Some days before the

Rising she wrote to the Chief Secretary appealing that efforts be made to solve Irish political difficulties by moderate and conciliatory methods, and by the avoidance of coercion, so as to 'save the country from an outbreak of violence that would be disastrous to her real interests and would create serious difficulties for the English government'.[30]

While fully committed to the internationalist ideal, Bennett was nevertheless convinced of the need for separate Irish representation at international feminist gatherings. She had first raised this issue in the spring of 1915 with the IWSA.[31] The Hague peace congress of that year saw the formation of an International Committee of Women for Permanent Peace (ICWPP). Subsequently a series of national committees was formed in Europe and the US. Initially Ireland was part of the British branch, and Bennett was the Irish representative on its executive. From the beginning she sought a separate Irish branch. A formal resolution to the ICWPP in October 1915 asked for independent representation for any nation feeling itself a distinct entity and enjoying or aspiring to enjoy self-government.[32] Expressing the discontent of Irish members, Bennett demanded that the principle of nationality should be clearly established in the constitution of the ICWPP, and that, 'the Committee shall act in accordance with their own resolution that autonomy shall not be refused to any people'. She pointed out that 'a branch of an English organisation is rarely, if ever, successful in Ireland. And in the matter of peace, the difficulties are intensified.'[33] In January 1916 the Irish branch took matters into its own hands, renaming its section the Irishwomen's International League (IIL). Prolonged and often bureaucratic correspondence with Head Office in Amsterdam on the issue continued through 1916. Bennett continued to make the point that it was not the number of representatives Ireland would be allowed on the International Committee that was at issue, but rather the principle of independent representation for Ireland. She emphasized that, 'The peace movement in Ireland must be indigenous and independent to be in any sense successful.'[34] The status of small and subject nations was discussed in depth by the ICWPP, and raised by Bennett at every international executive meeting. Strong support was given by the British branch – named the Women's International League (WIL), which late in 1916 stated:

> Unrest in Ireland we believe to be the result of tyranny and wrong, and the only way to peace is that of freedom and justice. So long as we deny these to Ireland we cannot expect that the rest of Europe will have much confidence in our desire to safeguard the rights of 'small nationalities'. We are proud to know that the Irishwomen's International League is

> standing bravely for *all* the ideals for which we are banded together – feminism, nationalism and inter-nationalism, peace and freedom.[35]

Confident that full national status would soon be granted, the IIL in October 1916 argued that its insistence on the practical recognition of the principle of nationality within the International Committee had:

> Done some service to the cause of Irish nationalism, and of nationalism all the world over. For we are helping to give Ireland international importance and responsibility by basing her claim for independence on a moral principle. The small and subject nations have world duties and world responsibilities, and at this time it ought to be the duty of a nation placed as Ireland is, to make her contribution to the cause of permanent international peace, by a clear and uncompromising advocacy of the principle of nationality.[36]

Finally, in December 1916, the IIL was formally accepted as an independent national organization.[37] A similar campaign had been waged by the IWSF within the international suffrage movement. Writing in 1917 to *Jus Suffragii,* its executive asked why Ireland was consistently omitted from the list of member countries published each month, commenting:

> Readers of your valued paper are thus given to suppose that Ireland is either a part of Great Britain or that she is non-existent. I hope that by publishing this letter you will allow me the opportunity of assuring them that neither of these suppositions is correct.[38]

This was to prove a more protracted campaign, as the constitution of the IWSA granted separate representation only to countries with independent powers of enfranchisement. National recognition was finally granted to Ireland within the IWSA in 1922.

During the early months of 1916, the IIL continued to work for the complete enfranchisement of women, and to foster co-operation with women of other countries in attaining permanent international peace. On the home front it pledged to work for 'a just and reasonable settlement of the Irish question by helping to promote goodwill and a better understanding between different sections of people in Ireland and by steadfastly opposing the use of destructive force by any section'.[39] Regular meetings were held to discuss the Hague resolutions and other topical issues arising from the war. Conscription was condemned, the right of small nationalities to independence was stressed and support was given to the establishment of a conference of neutral nations to facilitate a mediated settlement to the war. The formation of a League of Nations as proposed by President Wilson was strongly supported and the re-organization of Europe on the principle of nationality welcomed. Concepts of independence and nationality were to dominate Irish political life over the coming years, and groups such as the IIL would not be immune from friction over these issues.

The Easter Rising of 1916 – and the murder of Frank Sheehy Skeffington – placed immense strain on women's groups generally, and on pacifist groups in particular. Bennett, who took over Skeffington's mantle as *Irish Citizen* editor and pacifist voice, notified ICWPP headquarters that Irish members now had to concentrate on encouraging a more conciliatory spirit among the various sections of Irish life. Her personal views on independence for Ireland were stated quite clearly when she asked 'How far is it immoral, even criminal, to postpone practical recognition of the "sacred right of freedom" to this particular small nation of Ireland?'[40] The abandonment of an active suffrage campaign in Britain in favour of various war-works had prompted Bennett to describe English suffragists as 'a servile sex'. Noting that Irishwomen were more independent so far, she urged caution 'for our political women hang on blindly to their particular political half-good fetishes, whether Sinn Féin or Redmondites'. Documenting various committees with little representation of women, where male members made decisions regarding women's issues, Bennett wrote to Hanna Sheehy Skeffington in despair: 'There is no getting away from it, women in general are a poor crowd, willing to be under the thumb of men'.[41] In a letter to Lloyd George, John Redmond and other Irish politicians on behalf of the IIL, Bennett argued that:

> We hope presently to find Ireland playing a helpful part in a common effort of all civilised nations to set up such political machinery as will ensure permanent peace; and we therefore appeal to you to support now the claim of Irishwomen to representation in any system of Government which may be established as testimony that safe and constructive government must rest on right rather than might, on reason rather than on physical force.[42]

ICWPP records indicate that censorship fears prevented publication of this letter in their newsletter *International*. Following the IIL's first annual general meeting in January 1917, Bennett forwarded a statement to head-office in Amsterdam regarding recent declarations for a proposed League of Nations. Welcoming President Wilson's proposals to the

Allies in this regard, the statement noted:

> Such a re-organisation based upon the principle of nationality (by which we understand the recognition of an articulate demand on the part of any people for independence) can be brought about only by free discussion among the nations and requires for its realisation the co-operation and consent of all. As members of a small nation we have a special interest in this pronouncement of the Allies, and we trust that when the re-organisation of Europe is effected, the right of our own country to full and free development on the basis of nationality will be fully acknowledged.[43]

Despite the turbulent events of the previous year, this oblique reference was the only mention of political developments in Ireland in this first anniversary message. Some months later Bennett forwarded to the ICWPP executive in Amsterdam a number of resolutions passed at an IIL conference in Dublin for consideration in the post-war situation. These related to the spiritual purposes of humanity, women in public life, the rights of small nations, a League of Nations, and the responsibilities of the smaller nations. These resolutions not only indicate debate within the Irish branch, but, in particular, echo Bennett's thinking as reflected in her writing and correspondence now and in later years. Their assertion of the rights of small nations declared that, 'every people united by a conscious sense of nationality shall have the right to choose the government under which they shall live, and to determine their own way of development'.[44] Significantly, during 1918 the IIL's letterheading was changed to Gaelic with the English title in smaller print underneath.[45] Irish and English branches of ICWPP worked very closely during this period, particularly on the treatment of Irish political prisoners and on opposition to conscription in Ireland. In the autumn of 1918 Bennett was invited by the WIL executive to address a series of meetings throughout England. During this trip she managed to obtain a brief interview with David Lloyd George, the British Prime Minister, seeking the release of Irish prisoners. A report on her visit commented:

> A few more visitors like Miss Louie Bennett would do a power of good. Those who had the opportunity of hearing her speak at the 1917 Club and for the WIL will never again wonder at Ireland's intense nationality. She has shown too, that in Ireland the Trade Union Movement is far more than the mere demand for better wages and fairer hours, important as these are. The enthusiasm which blazes in the Labour Movement in Ireland is a revelation to people whose causes are for their spare moments.[46]

Charlotte Despard commented after hearing Bennett speak that Irish people 'would not now be satisfied with Home Rule. They desire to have their Nationality recognised.'[47] A special executive meeting of the WIL held the morning after Bennett's London appearance declared its shame that British statesmanship had left Ireland in the hands of an arbitrary, repressive, militarist government and called for the withdrawal of the military occupation of Ireland.[48]

During 1918 a number of war-related issues saw suffrage and other women's groups in Ireland organize in unison. Chief among these was the campaign against the proposed implementation of the Conscription Act to Ireland. The Irish Parliamentary Party voted against the measure and returned to Ireland in protest. Among the many meetings and conferences organised in protest against this proposal was a mass meeting of women at Dublin's Mansion House, at which all present pledged to resist conscription. A national women's day was organized during which women throughout the country pledged not to take jobs vacated by men who were conscripted. In Dublin along with representatives of various women's societies, Bennett led her union members in procession to the City Hall to sign this pledge.[49] The Conscription Act was not enforced in Ireland. Informing Amsterdam of the IIL's work in this successful campaign, Bennett wrote: 'We hope that the fact that Ireland has remained free from Conscription may help in securing freedom from it for all countries.' Pointing out that the IIL was now preoccupied with the problem of self-determination for Ireland, she noted: 'We desire to see President Wilson's principle in regard to government by consent fully applied in the case of the Irish nation.'[50]

In May 1919 the ICWPP held its second congress in Zurich. Plans to hold this post-war congress side by side with the official peace congress at Versailles had to be abandoned as delegates from the defeated powers were refused permission to enter France. Among the smaller countries represented for the first time was Ireland, with Louie Bennett as its delegate.[51] At this congress the ICWPP was renamed the Women's International League for Peace and Freedom (WILPF) and its headquarters moved to Geneva.[52] An 'Appeal On Behalf Of Ireland' issued to the congress by the Irish branch sought support for Ireland 'in her legitimate struggle for rights of self-determination'. This appeal asked delegates to

> Help us to regain our birthright, the right to meet and work with other Nations on an equal plane. We want, all of us, to regain it by honourable

> means. We can say of Dáil Éireann that it is on fire for justice, that it bears ill will to none, if only the alien government which crushes and oppresses the people could be ousted.[53]

An IIL post-congress document addressed 'To The Smaller Nations' pointed out that following the Versailles peace treaty such nations were now in greater peril than ever before, commenting that 'imperialism seems to have entrenched itself behind a travesty of the original conception of a League of Nations'. Signed by Louie Bennett, this document described nationality as 'a strong and indestructible human instinct, necessary as an incentive to progress, [but one which must be] closely allied with internationalism, as no nation may live for itself alone'. Calling on all smaller nations to make common cause with Ireland in an alliance of non-imperialistic peoples committed to self-determination, whose object would be a true League of Nations, Bennett wrote:

> We declare our belief that the fate of many other nations is involved in the fate of Ireland: her continued subjection will inevitably encourage further violations of fundamental principles of international morality; but her liberation would make a definite advance towards such a World Commonwealth as alone can promise equal security for all peoples. Therefore the liberation of Ireland is the concern of all who seek peace and freedom.[54]

These were tempestuous times for a pacifist organization. Bennett wrote to Emily Balch in October 1920: 'Things are very difficult here and we are hard put to it to keep our little group together. We are really living in a "war-zone" in Ireland, and our minds and hearts are racked daily.'[55] During 1920 Bennett and Balch corresponded regularly on the issue of passive resistance, to which both were committed. Bennett had been active in promoting the ideal of passive resistance from the time of the anti-conscription campaign, and had presented an outline for such a scheme to the Labour Party in December 1919. In March 1920, however, she informed Balch that passive resistance in Ireland had been engulfed in the terrible cyclone of force on all sides. She told Balch that she could make any use she wished of a memorandum Bennett had sent her on the subject, provided Balch did not mention that it was drafted by the Irish Labour Party. This would seem to underline Bennett's comments to Balch three months earlier, when she indicated that the Labour Party believed that the time had not yet arrived when it would be desirable for it to risk any publicity in this regard. Bennett was certain that a scheme of passive resistance could be devised, but was convinced that it must have an economic basis and be backed by the workers. Confirming the willingness of the Irish branch to provide material for Balch, Bennett pointed out that, 'It is practically impossible to do more than have a few conferences on the subject, as it seems a mockery to sit down and discuss it in cold blood in these days in Ireland.' Referring to the Irish experience of hunger strike, she stated:

> I do not think any nation would carry out a scheme of passive resistance unless they are inspired by an intense *spiritual* [*sic*] passion, a religious fervour that lifts the soul of the people. I believe that if the Irish Catholic Church had joined whole heartedly in this national struggle and come toward with a scheme of passive resistance, that it would have been done, and done successfully. I think and hope Ghandi is great enough to achieve something of this sort in India.[56]

Study of the early feminist movement in countries of mixed race has highlighted the white bourgeois background of many suffrage groups, often allied to racist views against extending suffrage to immigrants and blacks.[57] While this situation was not relevant in an Irish context, Bennett's correspondence with Emily Balch during 1920 includes one startling letter on the issue of race. Writing to Balch on behalf of the IIL in protest against the use of black troops in the French Army of occupation in Germany, Bennett stated:

> All civilised women will surely wish to unite in using their influence with the *Entente* to save German women and girls from the unspeakable horrors which such a system must create. We in Ireland who are living now under a Military Occupation of civilised white troops can well imagine the perils and terrors to which these German women must be subjected.[58]

Balch, in response, noted that countries such as France were allowed to enforce conscription in their colonies, a fact she described as an outrage against the native population as well as against the civilized world. She further pointed out that troops conscripted in this way were likely to be more docile and less apt to shrink from barbarities commanded or committed on their own initiative than 'civilized' soldiers, commenting: 'When one thinks what orders civilised soldiers will obey, and what they will do without orders or contrary to orders, the prospect is not a pleasant one.'[59] While such views would appear to conflict with Bennett's championing of equality, it is clear that this particular issue was a cause of discussion and concern among branches of WILPF during these years.[60]

Despite often radically different political loyalties, women's groups in Ireland joined together to campaign on a number of controversial issues from 1918. In addition to the anti-conscription campaign, women's groups also protested against the implementation of Regulation 40D under the Defence of the Realm Act (DORA). The introduction of Regulation 40D was seen as an attempt to revive the notorious Contagious Diseases Acts which had been repealed in 1886 following strenuous agitation by suffragists in Ireland and England. A further remarkable example of joint action occurred in 1919 with an 'Appeal on Behalf of the Principal Women's Associations of Ireland' to their sisters in other countries to demand the establishment of an international committee of inquiry into the conditions of Irish political prisoners. In sending a draft of this petition to Geneva in November 1919, Bennett explained that it was to be signed on behalf of four women's organizations 'who realised that the subject of political and war prisoners is one that is striking the hearts of many women in many countries'.[61] The following month, however, she asked Geneva not to publish the petition for the moment as 'there had been a little difficulty about signatures'. That there were some initial differences among signatories is not surprising when one notes that they included Constance de Markievicz, Hanna Sheehy Skeffington, Maud Gonne MacBride and Bennett herself. By January 1920 these difficulties were sorted out, and the petition was forwarded. It was argued that should England refuse to allow what France, Germany, Austria and Italy had willingly accepted, her government would stand self-condemned. Outlining the loss of free speech and press under English military rule, it concluded with an appeal to the civilized world to 'break down the wall of silence with which England seeks to surround Ireland'.[62]

In the autumn of 1920 the Manchester branch of the WIL organized a fact-finding trip to Ireland to investigate conditions. A report of their findings was published and a series of public meetings was held throughout England. Audiences were shown 'magic-lantern' slides of photographs taken during the trip, showing ruined homes, wrecked shops and buildings.[63] At all of these meetings resolutions were passed and forwarded to the government demanding the liberation of prisoners and a truce during which Irish people might determine their own form of government. This report formed the basis for extensive propaganda by the British and Irish WILPF in conjunction with other national sections. In the United States, Jane Addams and Emily Balch were among those who responded. Prior to the British WIL trip, Bennett had sent a cable to Addams in Chicago asking that, 'Irish Woman Workers and International League beg American women urge Presidents intervention on behalf Irish prisoners dying for their political faith.'[64] As a result of such pressure a lobby of Congress and a commission of inquiry into Irish affairs were established. A broad cross-section of interests was included on this commission – senators, congressmen, mayors, governors, trade unionists and WILPF president Jane Addams. In January 1921 Bennett and Caroline Townshend (an officer of the Gaelic League) travelled to Washington as IIL delegates.[65] Bennett's evidence to the commission runs over some sixty-five pages of the official report, and covers a wide range of issues from the state of Irish industry, attacks on co-operative initiatives and maltreatment of the Catholic Church by Crown forces. It contains details on republican arbitration courts, the trade union and labour movements, murders and attacks on Irish civilians. While the IIL stance in Washington concentrated on the constructive activities of Dáil Éireann, rather than a chronicle of atrocities, Bennett's evidence makes it clear that atrocities and suppression had occurred. Introducing her testimony on behalf of the IIL, Bennett explained:

> There are going on at the present time two lines of conflict: there is the conflict between the Irish Government, the Dáil, and the British Government, along what one might call civil lines; and there is also the physical conflict, the conflict between the two armies. We thought it would be interesting to lay before your Commission facts in regard to the way in which the British Government have tried to block all the efforts of the Irish to establish or carry on industry, and to carry on their own local councils [and] their own courts of law as established by the Dáil.[66]

In the course of her evidence and questioning, Bennett's personal views on many of these issues emerge. Some members of the commission were puzzled by the fact that a Protestant woman could be acceptable as organiser of a trade union whose membership was primarily Catholic. Bennett assured them that she had found no antagonism whatsoever in this regard, although she confessed that when she first became involved she feared there might be some opposition.[67] With members of the Irish Women Workers' Union numbering six thousand, she noted that only about six of these were Protestant. Detailing the low wages paid to women workers, and the scandalous wages and living conditions of workers generally, she argued that, 'the industrial conditions in Dublin had a great deal to do with the uprising of 1916'. On a personal note she commented that, 'My Father was of the employing class, and they looked upon me as a sort of blackleg'.[68] Regarding attempts to curb the development of co-operatives, she believed there was a desire among the capitalist class in England to get Ireland in its grasp economically; the co-operative movement therefore was opposed because its success meant the destruction of capitalism.

Questioned about her own political affiliations, Bennett replied that she was not involved in any political work. When asked if she were republican in sympathy, she replied 'Yes, I am.'[69] Her evidence shows her to be most supportive of the republican court system established by the Dáil, pointing out however that these courts had been driven underground by the British government. In her evidence she noted that she had been asked to serve on one such court in the spring of 1920. She pointed out that Unionists too had come before these courts, and had spoken in the highest praise of the justice dispensed. Regarding the strength of the labour movement in Ireland, she considered it difficult to assess. While the leaders had a progressive socialistic programme in mind, this could not be promoted at present because of the absorption of the rank and file with the political question. Regarding the treatment given the Catholic Church by Crown forces, Bennett detailed instances of raids on monasteries and convents, arrests of priests and attacks on young men leaving mass. Commenting that it looked as if the authorities were deliberately trying to create a religious war, she explained that the ordinary people had coped with these trials through intense religious devotion. Making it clear she was not talking about the 'organized' Catholic Church, she gave an example close to her own home in Dublin during the MacSwiney hunger strike. In many areas, where priests were not in favour of Sinn Féin, ordinary people met to pray together. Such was the case in Killiney, where the priest did not want to hold a meeting. The local people met together and recited the rosary, and finally the curate came down and joined them.[70] Bennett listed the total number of men, women and children murdered in Ireland during 1920 as 203, (none of which occurred in armed conflict). She commented, 'They say they are shot trying to escape, but that is all humbug.'[71]

Bennett read to the commission a formal statement prepared by the IIL. The first paragraph stated:

> The Irishwomen's International League affirms that the responsibility for the bloodshed and violence in Ireland rests upon the British

> Government, which refused to allow her the indefeasible right of all nations to freedom, outlaws her duly elected Parliament, and persistently attempts to rule the people by force.

In conclusion, the statement declared:

> The Irish people have proved how unconquerable is the spirit of nationality. The peace and happiness of the world depend upon the measure of freedom given to that spirit. If Ireland wins her freedom now, the world will see a triumph of spiritual over material forces, and may look forward to the future with a diminished dread of devastating wars.[72]

From a somewhat different perspective, Mary and Muriel MacSwiney also gave evidence to the Washington commission. Aware of the importance of women's role in the Irish national movement, Cumann na mBan instructed MacSwiney in her subsequent tour of the US to assure Americans that 'The women of Ireland are standing with the soldiers and that, "no surrender" is the watchword.' MacSwiney's biographer notes that, 'the organisation did not want women represented as a pacifist group urging the men to lay down their arms.'[73] A broadsheet published at about this time, *Irishwomen and the Irish Republican Army*, emphasized that Irishwomen were as proud of their national army as women of other countries were of theirs and ranked them with the world's bravest. The document concluded:

> The women of Ireland consider it a crime for any young Irishman of military age *not* to carry arms in the defence of his country, and that it is an even greater crime for any person of Irish blood to refuse to harbour and assist our brave soldiers.[74]

Writing privately to Emily Balch, Bennett commented, 'I urged any groups of women I met in America to make this question of Ireland a moral rather than a political issue, so that it may be in some sense released from the entanglement of the anti-British movement in the States.'[75] Irish government awareness of WILPF activities has been documented in a recent publication on Irish foreign policy between 1919 and 1922. Writing to Eamon de Valera in 1919, representatives of Dáil Éireann who were in Paris for the Allied peace conference – ever mindful of Ireland's need for international support – expressed the hope that Bennett would call on them on her way back from Zurich.[76] In 1921, Harry Boland pointed out to de Valera that WILPF's president, Jane Addams, likely to be a member of an American delegation on disarmament, was also a member of the committee investigating conditions in Ireland.[77]

Acceptance of the Treaty by Dáil Éireann and the ensuing civil war had profound effects both on the IIL organization and on individual members attempting to ally pacifist convictions with political commitment. In her diaries Rosamund Jacob recorded discussions with Bennett about the Treaty and Document No. 2, which she noted Bennett despised.[78] With the lack of insight of one observing events from a distance, WILPF head-office believed that acceptance of the Treaty meant that Ireland could put the nightmare of violence and outrage behind it.[79] Explaining that in fact the Treaty was not popular and was reluctantly accepted, Bennett argued that there was much grief and shame about it amongst a very large 'minority'. She asked Emily Balch:

> Can you be surprised? We are asked to accept Common Citizenship with an Empire whose deeds we loathe – an Empire which today holds down Egypt and India as it has till now held down Ireland. There are men and women who could not take the oath of allegiance without sacrificing every instinct of honour in their nature.

She hoped that de Valera would be strong enough to lead his followers away from political division and concentrate on education and economic reconstruction, but she was unsure, noting that:

> The women here are a dangerous element – fierce, vindictive, without any constructive ability but with immense ability for obstruction and destructive tactics. A healthy opposition to the Free State would be excellent, without it Ireland may become as materialistic as England.

Her reservations regarding the attitude of women in the republican movement would be repeated later in 1922 with regard to the Irish Labour Party, which will be discussed below, and over the coming years within WILPF in Ireland.

Bennett explained to Balch that she did not fear injustice to religious or political minorities, but hatred of England could not disappear overnight. She pointed to consistent degradation by English armed forces of Irish men and women over the past two years. She was moved to state that:

> Nothing is so hard to forgive as degradation, and in these past two years the English armed forces have very literally forced Irish men and women to lick the dust. Men and boys who have been cruelly beaten, held up to

> the mockery and torment of a mob, tortured to betray their own people or forswear their own convictions – will never forgive or forget. It is not in human nature. To be honest, I hate England myself – not alone for what she has done to the Irish people, but for what she has done or consented to in Europe. The English people are a terrible people – I shrink from them in horror – but all the more I admire beyond words the magnificent exceptions amongst them – our own International women in especial.[80]

Within weeks of writing this letter Bennett was ordered to rest for two months due to heart problems – a result perhaps of her hectic and stressful lifestyle over the past decade. Commenting that 'It's hard to be quiet in this country!', Bennett could not remain entirely idle, and continued to correspond with Geneva. In particular she wrote on an issue dear to her heart, that of passive resistance. Noting that this subject was listed on WILPF's executive agenda, she informed Emily Balch that while failing energies had prevented her writing before on this topic, such was her interest that she had now gathered her thoughts on the subject. In the resulting document she stated that pacifism must be based on a religious principle, and means must be found to revive a sense of the sanctity of life.

> In advocating passive resistance we must be inspired by a religious sense of the value of life. Before we can hope to supersede militarism and faith in violence, we have got to convince men and women, of the religious value of life and therefore of man's indefeasible right to it. This surely is the modern woman's greatest duty?

She cited Gandhi and the English conscientious objectors as having made a valuable contribution to the promotion of passive resistance. Within an Irish context, while she accepted that passive resistance had only been used in conjunction with violence, she felt that a much greater victory could have been obtained by an exclusive use of the former. She listed the establishment of Sinn Féin government departments, law courts, councils and boards as having reduced British government to an absurdity, in spite of their military power of repression. She argued that if such methods were extended (through use of hunger-strike, boycott of English goods and tax-resistance), 'such tactics must bring a complete *impasse* in a short time. Then it becomes a test of endurance. Passive resistance must be preached before it is practised.'[81]

In June 1922 Bennett wrote to Sir James Craig appealing against the use of force and coercion in Belfast. Declaring the futility of using a partisan police force as a means of securing order, and asserting that lasting peace could never be secured by violence, her letter stated:

> We believe that a solution of the present tragic problem can only be found through negotiations with the Government of southern Ireland, and we therefore earnestly appeal to you, in the interests of civilisation, to enter into such negotiations, and to arrange for a truce while they continue. Sooner or later, negotiations must begin. We beg you to let them begin now.[82]

When simmering post-Treaty tensions finally escalated into civil war in June 1922, Bennett with Mary O'Connor of the IWWU set about trying to evacuate families living in the vicinity of the Four Courts. The Minister for Defence was petitioned to allow women and children in the danger zone to be re-housed in empty homes, and to be supplied with foodstuffs. A group of concerned women representing labour, nationalists and former suffragists met in Dublin's Mansion House to co-ordinate peace efforts. Two delegations were picked to present peace proposals to leaders on both sides. Bennett was the only one included in both delegations. The first delegation, received in Government Buildings by Michael Collins, Arthur Griffith and William T. Cosgrave, was told that there could be no truce until anti-government forces surrendered their arms. The second delegation to the republican side was informed of the latter's refusal to negotiate on any terms.[83] Three months later Bennett again tried to intercede, seeking an interview with the Minister for Defence, Richard Mulcahy, which was declined. Following these attempts to secure a cessation of hostilities, a Manifesto of Condemnation was issued by the IIL which was refused publication by the press and consequently was posted up in Dublin by the women themselves.[84] Later in the year the IWWU issued a manifesto asking leaders on both sides to state publicly their willingness to accept an unconditional truce, declaring: 'We are sick of battles, and bloodshed and terror. We want peace: we want work: we want security of life and home.[85]

The IIL was experiencing its own civil war at this time. Bennett informed Geneva of its impending dissolution, explaining that its existence over the past two years had been precarious and unsatisfactory for those who tried to be consistently pacifist.

> The civil strife in Ireland in the last few months has driven the larger majority of people into one or other political camp: both sides have raised objections to the attitude of the I.I.L.[86]

The success of the IIL in raising public awareness in England and the US on the issue of Irish political affairs may in fact have contributed to this crisis. Women like Hanna Sheehy Skeffington and Rosamund Jacob – long associated with the League – had become increasingly republican in attitude. Lucy Kingston noted that its 1920 packed annual general meeting showed 'great attendance of S.F.s [Sinn Féiners] including Gonne McBride, Capt. W. Mrs S.S. [Sheehy Skeffington] etc'.[87] Describing one of the Mansion House conference peace meetings chaired by Bennett in the summer of 1922, Jacob noted that it was attended by 'great crowds of women but none of them apparently really keen on peace'. Expecting that all speakers would be republicans, the audience in protest started singing a hymn to the Queen of Heaven, a development which Jacob observed 'Miss Bennett received awfully well'.[88] As a result of political differences this Peace Conference of Women ultimately collapsed. Bennett informed Geneva:

> The Republican section of this conference drifted into party propaganda, especially in regard to the prisoners . . . the Free State element in the I.I.L. have, almost to a woman, resigned on account of our association with the Mansion House Conference.[89]

Bennett still felt that they were right to have tried. She also felt, however, that the time had come for radical changes within the IIL. She suggested a new Irish section of WILPF be started under new influence, commenting, 'Miss Jacob is too Republican, I am too actively connected with Labour, to be anything but a danger to the sort of organisation that is needed.' Arguing the necessity of maintaining an all-Ireland society – 'to maintain social links and to obliterate the ugly antagonism now existing', she disagreed with Geneva's proposal for a separate northern section, stating that this would make the process of reconciliation even more difficult. Reflecting the turmoil and crises of conscience experienced by pacifists throughout Europe in recent years, even Bennett's convictions were shaken, as she confessed to Balch:

> All that has happened and is still happening here drives one to review very seriously one's attitude to pacifism. I am driven to think that some forms of anarchy can only be dealt with by the use of force. When accepted moral standards break down, what is to be done to secure innocent people from cruelty and loss of life and property?

Within a few days of receiving this letter a committee meeting of the IIL decided to keep the group going for the moment, with Rosamund Jacob taking over as secretary *pro-tem* from Bennett. Two weeks later at its annual general meeting Bennett formally resigned as secretary, warning the group against allowing on its committee 'women who take prominent place in contemporary politics'.[90] However, the new committee for 1922-3 did include many high-profile political women. Charlotte Despard was its chair, at the same time being chair of the Women's Prisoners Defence Association (formed in 1922 with Maud Gonne MacBride). Rosamund Jacob, Hanna Sheehy Skeffington and Maud Gonne MacBride were also much involved.

Not surprisingly, such a volatile committee led to numerous incidents of disagreement. One such incident occurred in January 1923 when Rosamund Jacob was arrested and imprisoned for allowing republicans the use of Hanna Sheehy Skeffington's house. Lucy Kingston commented tartly that, while Sheehy Skeffington would undoubtedly have agreed with Jacob's action, it was somewhat rash of Jacob considering her role within the IIL, noting, 'we are not benefitted in any way by having our Secretary in prison'.[91] Kingston's diary also reveals that the issue of Charlotte Despard's resignation was raised more than once, each time Despard declaring herself a pacifist and neutral regarding government. Kingston was relieved that Mrs Dix was joint secretary, 'she is sane and thoroughly pacifist and does not stink in the eyes of government like Mrs D[espard] and Mme. G. McB'. Early in 1923 a special meeting was called to consider the following resolution by Louie Bennett:

> That membership of the Irish Section is open to all who hold that in resisting tyranny or striving for freedom only such methods may be used as will not involve the taking of life.[92]

In a country in the midst of civil war, this resolution stripped the *raison d'être* from a group such as the IIL. After heated discussion it was rejected by just one vote. The issue of the legitimate use of force remained a thorny one and would continue to dog the IIL during its remaining years. For the moment the League survived, noting in its annual report that, 'taking into account the terrible crisis through which the country is passing, we have not done too badly'.[93] Over the next two years Bennett disappears from IIL and WILPF records, although indications are that she remained a member. Lucy Kingston and Rosamund Jacob represented Ireland at the Third International Congress in Vienna in June 1921, while Marie Johnson filled that role in Washington in 1924. Johnson was happy to tell the Congress that Ireland now had full adult suffrage.[94]

In 1925 the IIL invited the international executive of WILPF to hold its Fifth International Congress in Dublin the following year. The invitation was enthusiastically accepted. It was seen by Jane Addams and her executive as an 'extended peace mission'. Its official history notes that:

> The choice owed something to the courageous stand for non-violence of Louie Bennett and her co-workers, as well as to the tragic situation of Ireland itself.[95]

Bennett had always been highly regarded by the WILPF executive, and from early 1926 she features regularly in correspondence regarding the forthcoming congress. In the work of organization she was assisted by a committee of eleven, with Rosamund Jacob, Lucy Kingston and Helen Chenevix playing key roles.[96] And it was quite a mammoth task for a small national section to undertake. Interesting details emerge from correspondence between Dublin and Geneva over these months with the Irish section advising on sensitive political issues, protocol and customs. The problem of location was solved when the organizing committee managed to obtain the use of National University buildings in Dublin. Lucy Kingston informed Geneva that the government had at last realized the importance of bringing so many visitors to Dublin, although she cautioned, 'we are careful . . . not to put our Branch too greatly under the Government "wing". This would incriminate our League with a certain section of the public.'[97] Bennett further warned Geneva to exercise caution in press notices regarding conditions under which the National University was obtained for the congress, pointing out that the university president alone had authority to allow the use of college buildings, and emphasizing:

> *The Government have nothing whatever to do with it.* See to it that in all public notices he is given credit for lending it, and that no whisper of Government aid is made. This is very important.[98]

Under the pressure of organizing such a big event, old tensions re-emerged. Lucy Kingston recorded her annoyance with Bennett on a number of occasions in the lead up to the congress, finding her hard to work with and inclined to innuendo. Confirmation of such tensions recur in Bennett's remarks to Madeleine Doty on 'the struggle of making an amateur Committee realise the value of order & efficient office administration!'[99] In contrast, Jacob's diaries claim that, 'Louie B.

is a great help, though Lucy thinks her a steamroller.' Jacob subsequently discussed the matter with Bennett, noting that the latter 'knows she is a "steamroller" – I'm sure she has to be with the Union people'.[100] Writing to one of the WILPF executive travelling to Ireland ahead of the conference to put final touches in place, Bennett advised:

> There is one point I must impress on you. Ireland is not at all American in method. We are leisurely people and we rarely manage to get things successfully done in a hurry. So don't build on rushing everything through when you come here.[101]

Kingston's suggestion that a commemorative stamp be printed with the date and place of congress was greeted enthusiastically by Geneva, as was Bennett's suggestion of a poster designed by a well-known artist to advertise the congress. She informed Geneva that she hoped to obtain such a design from Jack Yeats. The latter was not confirmed in subsequent correspondence, although orders for both a poster and stamps were placed by WILPF branches. Unfortunately, the only extant record of either is a photocopy of the commemorative stamp on an IIL letter to Geneva. Correspondence between Dublin and Geneva during this time indicates that Bennett hoped that Gandhi might attend the Dublin conference, a hope that did not materialize due to the latter's illness.

The congress, which took place between 8 and 15 July 1926, was attended by 150 delegates representing twenty countries. This was the first gathering of an international organization to be held in the Irish Free State since its recognition by Britain in 1921. A reception to mark its opening was attended by both Eamon de Valera and W.T. Cosgrave. This first public function attended by both leaders since the civil war naturally attracted much comment. R.M. Fox recounts that when Bennett concluded her opening address to the conference by inviting the 'president' to say a few words:

> The two rival groups in front of the platform stiffened and glared defiantly at each other. Everyone waited breathlessly to see which of the two Presidents would step up and speak in the name of the country. But as Louie Bennett disappeared from view, there mounted in her place, a third President, a small grey-haired, determined looking woman – Jane Addams, the President of the International League for Peace and Freedom. So the moment of tension passed.[102]

However apocryphal this account may be, records show that there had been a series of meetings between de Valera and Rosamund Jacob of the

IIL in the previous months. De Valera had indicated that he would not meet members of the Free State government socially, but he would meet them in business assemblies. It would appear that he thought it strange that Dr Coffey and he were not asked to speak and welcome the delegates. Jacob pointed out to him that this would not fit in with the non-political ideals of the committee. Consistently, during her interviews with de Valera, Jacob pointed out that if republicans did not participate in the conference, the government side would gain sole access to foreign delegates. That her strategy worked was confirmed when de Valera promised to publish any pre-conference material in *An Phoblacht,* and to attend the conference opening. Subsequently he attended a post-conference party, at which Jacob noted he was surrounded by a circle of delegates who were listening to him and arguing with him.[103]

The congress was a great success, particularly with the Dublin press, which assiduously covered both its working sessions and its many social functions. Among these was a garden party given by the Governor-General at the Vice-Regal Lodge, whose guest list spanned a broad range of Irish political, literary and social life. Jacob noted that Bennett opted not to attend this event – an action disapproved of by her mother. But the work of the congress was very serious. Within an overall theme of 'Next Steps towards Peace', plenary sessions included speakers and discussion on colonial and economic imperialism, women and world peace, relation of majorities and minorities, conciliation, arbitration and disarmament. Addressing the congress, Ronald J.P. Mortished, Assistant Secretary of the Irish Labour Party, admitted that Ireland could scarcely claim to have either an international or pacifist outlook. He noted however that the WIL 'has come to us with a magnificent defiance of the destructive power of hate and a magnificent faith in the power of love informed by intelligence'.[104]

A public meeting was held in the Mansion House under the auspices of the conference on the theme 'Next Steps towards World Peace'. The title had been amended on the advice of Bennett to Geneva because 'we think the word world essential in view of our faction fights here'. Some two thousand people are reported to have attended this event, which was chaired by Bennett. At this meeting Jane Addams spoke of the great Irish pacifist of international repute, Frank Sheehy Skeffington. Quoting Skeffington, 'I advocate no mere slavish acceptance of injustice. I am, and always will be, a fighter,' Addams highlighted WILPF's agreement with his appeal for new methods free from physical violence for ending struggle.[105] (Jacob claimed that all the papers deliberately omitted this quote.) In reply, Hanna Sheehy Skeffington, representing the republican group, thanked Addams for her tribute to her late husband and urged the WILPF to continue its stress on peace and freedom, quoting Pearse, 'Ireland unfree can never be at peace'. She felt it most appropriate that the congress met in Ireland 'because Ireland is the country that knows most what foreign violence and militarism mean'. Her speech aroused great enthusiasm. Jacob noted in her diary:

> When Hanna rose to second the vote of thanks, a roar of applause broke out for all the world as if it was de Valera, and went on and on and on (with cries of up the Republic) till Louie got quite annoyed with the enthusiasm and demanded 'Will you let Mrs Skeffington speak!'[106]

Jacob commented that she had seldom enjoyed an occasion more, noting that Sheehy Skeffington had got in some good punches, praising Jane Addams as chairman of the 1920–21 commission 'whose evidence was and I believe still is seditious literature in Ireland'. Skeffington went on to state how easy it was to be a pacifist in time of peace in comparison with wartime conditions. Interestingly, neither Sheehy Skeffington's reception nor the latter two quotations from her speech were printed in the official report of the congress. Writing of Bennett's life thirty years later, R.M. Fox commented of the incident, 'One could sense the emotional pull between the pacifist and militant Republicans, who were still unreconciled to peaceful methods.'[107]

One of the British speakers at the congress, Helena Swanwick, related how dissident members of Irish WILPF ('The Black women') remained outside the conference because they had taken part in the civil war and were still involved with revolutionary republicans. She noted that in several European countries including Ireland, 'The necessity for catastrophic revolution is maintained by those who are united in their opposition to international wars. They seem to me to be opportunists, because they drop their principle when it inconveniences them.'[108] And there was criticism for such action from other quarters. The *International Woman Suffrage News,* complimenting the Irish committee for a successful congress, noted that the 'only regrettable feature was the use made of the Congress as a platform for intense nationalist propaganda. We feel [this is] a misuse of what should be purely international and pacifist.'[109] It is clear from correspondence between Geneva headquarters and Louie Bennett that there was unease at such incidents. Neither the official WILPF report of the congress nor its Journal, *Pax International,* mentioned these issues, but praised the Irish section for its efficiency and hospitality, and its tact in getting all parties together. In particular they complimented Bennett for her poise, tolerance and quiet strength.

Bennett was elected to the executive committee of WILPF at this congress. This was not enough to endear her to Lucy Kingston, whose assessment was that Rosamund Jacob 'stands the test of the Congress well and Miss B[ennett] badly – uprisings of egotism again'.[110] There appears no doubt that Bennett was tough to work with, and did not hesitate to criticize where she thought it deserved. Only months after the Dublin congress she wrote sharply to Madeleine Doty in Geneva, complaining that members of the executive committee had been treated with extraordinary discourtesy because they had not all been informed of the time and place of the executive meeting until the latter was actually taking place. Bennett left Doty in no doubt about her feelings:

> Candidly I should not care to remain a member of the Executive, if its business is conducted on such lines. With a scattered organisation such as the W.I.L. strict business methods at Head Quarters are absolutely essential. You must forgive me for criticising you. I must criticise if I see or imagine the need of it.[111]

The reverberation of republican actions during the Dublin congress was remembered in the lead up to WILPF's 1929 Congress in Prague. Mary Sheepshanks (International Secretary WILPF) confessed to Bennett:

> The prospect of having those Republicans at Prague fills me with dismay. They did their best to spoil the Dublin Congress and did succeed in doing a certain amount of mischief . . . I thought they were so bitter and unscrupulous and unfair in their statements, and of course, many of the Germans and Americans were entirely taken in by them. I do hope you can do something to keep them off Prague.[112]

From this correspondence it is clear that there were some lively meetings of the IIL in the months before Prague. Bennett had been particularly busy with trade union commitments from 1928. This, allied to ongoing health problems, had caused her to miss many meetings of the IIL. That there was disquiet within the IIL committee because of this was articulated by Kingston's diary entry in July 1929 noting that they were about to pass a vote of protest at Bennett's absences. Likewise, Una Dix informed head-office that Bennett had virtually ignored the IIL during 1929, even though she was its president, and had not attended a special meeting called ahead of the Prague congress to discuss her proposed paper. Back in August of the previous year, Bennett had apologized to head-office in Geneva for not writing on several matters, explaining:

> I have been completely tied up this summer with Trade Union business, and it is literally true that I have not been able to take one day off duty during this summer. And as I have also had many family difficulties to meet, it has been quite impossible to give any time to W.I.L. work – very much to my regret.[113]

Records show that she was indeed very much occupied during the latter half of 1928. From June to October she was involved in a strike of women box-makers in Dublin, and during this period her mother was seriously ill. Bennett was forced to miss an executive meeting in April 1929 due to her mother's illness, but by July 1929 her mother had rallied sufficiently that she wrote to Sheepshanks in Geneva:

> I hope I may go to Prague with a comparatively easy mind. I have lived for years in a constant conflict of mind regarding the call of home and public duties. I want so much to be at the Prague Congress that this time I have resolved to take risks about home.[114]

Irish delegates to Prague were to be Bennett, Hanna Sheehy Skeffington and Rosamund Jacob. At the last minute Bennett could not travel because her mother's condition had deteriorated, but she forwarded a copy of a paper she had been asked to present on 'The Machinery of Internal Peace'. Bennett had informed Geneva that she would prefer not to speak on the political aspects of the subject but, rather, on the industrial aspects. A copy of this paper came to the attention of Sinn Féin, whose publication of extracts and hostile editorial comments plunged the IIL once more into fierce controversy. Sinn Féin wrote to WILPF in Geneva taking issue with Bennett's 'misleading & prejudicial comments regarding the state of government in Ireland'. It was claimed that she had accused Sinn Féin of attracting young people of an adventurous spirit as well as cranks, vagabonds and villains, commenting that, 'An irregular minority of this sort inspires fear in Government and constitutional circles'. Outlining a resulting vicious circle of arrests, victimization, terrorism and reprisals, Bennett had stated that while Sinn Féin was not in sympathy with the ideals of Labour, it would not hesitate to use it to secure the complete independence of Ireland. She commented:

> In Ireland, as elsewhere, the Communist is endeavouring to exploit nationalism (in its Republican cloak) for his own economic ends. It is

> unlikely that Communism will ever gain any real economic hold on Ireland; but it can add zest and money to the Republican forces. Working class discontent is a peculiarly dangerous element in a country where there is a political minority which refuses constitutional representation and looks to revolution as the means of emancipation.

Angrily refuting Bennett's implications regarding funding, Sinn Féin declared that it had more genuine sympathy with the ideals of Labour than all the time-servers who exploited the working-class cause. Criticizing official Labour for succumbing to temptation, accepting senatorial sinecures, and climbing on the shoulders of the workers to positions of emolument, Sinn Féin's letter noted that:

> Miss Bennett's assumption of an inherent right to voice the ideals of Labour is only less farcical than the posturings of the titled personages who pollute the English Labour movement.[115]

Despite Bennett's somewhat haughty remark to Geneva that she had disregarded Sinn Féin's letter as unworthy of notice, the Irish section was thrown into turmoil as a result of this controversy. At its next committee meeting, Lucy Kingston noted: 'L.B. is attacked for her paper by (1) S.Fein (2) Fianna Fail (3) Republ. members of our Committee. Find myself on her side for once, and certainly Mrs S.S.[Sheehy Skeffington] and the rest shew no mercy . . . An implacable crew where "The Rock of the Republic" is concerned.'[116] Bennett further informed Geneva that Hanna Sheehy Skeffington was particularly enraged:

> All through the past year there has been considerable dissatisfaction amongst the really pacifist group, owing to the presence on the Committee of people who openly state that they consider the use of force essential to achieve a social revolution, or to achieve national freedom. They lay emphasis on the W.I.L. object of *freedom* rather than peace . . . Things have now reached a climax . . . and I think a split is inevitable.[117]

The situation outlined by Bennett had been complicated further by the recent election of Maud Gonne MacBride to the IIL committee. Its then Secretary, Una M'Clintock Dix, had explained to Geneva:

> Realising that a peace committee with Mme MacBride on it was farce I wrote to her privately asking her to resign. She refused after consulting Mrs Sheehy Skeffington saying it would not be fair to those who elected her.[118]

A series of stormy committee meetings ensued, with debate centering on acceptance or rejection of the Washington Object that excluded from membership those who justified defensive warfare and armed revolution. A majority decision in favour of the Object was subsequently amended by a smaller gathering. Bennett and Chenevix were among those who then resigned from the committee, with Bennett informing Geneva that both felt it essential that the Irish branch be purged of political opportunists. Kingston noted that this was 'the saddest W.I.L. Cte. I ever attended'.[119] Although Dix disliked this show of sharp practice, she acknowledged that it provided a way out of their dilemma and enabled the group to remain in existence – however precariously.

Another significant factor in the *impasse* which was noted by Dix was the clash between the strong personalities of Bennett and Sheehy Skeffington.[120] WILPF's Geneva office viewed the matter most seriously, placing it on its executive agenda and pointing out that any serious dissension within a national branch was a source of concern for the whole league. However, by spring 1930 the group appeared to have weathered the storm. Its AGM voted to return to the Washington Object, and many former members rejoined, including Bennett. Informing Geneva that she had rejoined as a passive member, but that Helen Chenevix remained outside as she could not accept their illogical position, Bennett commented, 'This affords me intense amusement, as I am always held to be the wicked one who leads Helen into rebellious conduct.'[121] Within a few months, however, a further controversy would prove fatal. From October 1930, IIL members had been collecting signatures for a disarmament declaration initiated by WILPF. In the spring of 1931 the IIL, in association with the League of Nations Society, organized a public meeting to debate the issue. It was decided to invite as guest speaker Patrick McGilligan who was Minister for External Affairs in the Free State government. This choice of speaker naturally caused uproar among a section of the committee – partly because of McGilligan's political identity, and partly because he had been a member of the government which had executed republican leaders. Others felt that such objections were politically sectarian, and that McGilligan should be heard. On losing a subsequent vote to rescind the invitation, a number of members announced their intention to disrupt the meeting. The proposed meeting was subsequently cancelled with both the president and secretary resigning in protest. Rosamund Jacob wrote to Geneva desperately trying to retain some WILPF presence in Ireland, asking if there were precedent for two groups to operate within one section where controversial matters arose. Explaining this specific incident she informed Geneva that:

> The upshot of the affair is that the cleavage which has always existed in our Section has become so definite that we are in danger of a break-up, unless some new method of organisation can be devised. I think the clearest way to describe the cleavage is to say that some of us would put peace before freedom, and others would put freedom before peace.[122]

Despite Jacob's efforts, the groups did disintegrate at this point. Many former members had become active in the disarmament movement and were not anxious – and one gathers had not the heart nor energy – to continue reeling from one destructive split to another. Involvement in the disarmament campaign provided many women with a means to remain involved in the peace movement without engaging in divisive political arguments. The issue of 'justifiable warfare' caused dissension in many national sections of WILPF – up to and after the Second World War. Ireland in the 1920s was a country recently emerged from insurrection and civil war, where political division was still a fresh wound, and where many women still believed that the struggle for national independence was not yet complete. While condemning militarism in its imperialistic mode, some justified the need for further military action to attain national objectives. Others within the Irish WILPF could not accept such views.

In his examination of European feminist and socialist women's opposition to the First World War, Richard Evans details the overwhelming support of the war by feminists throughout Europe, commenting that 'Feminist pacifism [became] the creed of a minority, of a tiny band of courageous and principled women on the far-left fringes of bourgeois-liberal feminism.' Arguing that the 'first-wave' European feminism of the late nineteenth century was closely connected with the ideology of bourgeois nationalism, Evans notes that in some countries 'feminists identified with the movement for national self-determination to such an extent that nationalist aims almost took precedence over feminists ones'. By the early 1900s however, he notes, the connection between nationalism and feminism was being challenged by a minority of pacifists within the feminist movement, while an even larger group of socialist women rejected accepted notions of the female character and mission, arguing for the primacy of class consciousness and proletarian solidarity. Evans argues that any connection between pacifism and feminism was political and ideological, not 'natural' or inevitable. Noting that pacifists tended to come from a limited but distinct strand of feminist ideology on the democratic left of the movement, he concludes that 'the views of the feminist pacifists were limited in their appeal because the historical links between nationalism and feminism were still strong in the late nineteenth and early twentieth centuries'.[123]

It would be almost sixty years before a WILPF branch was re-established in Ireland.[124] Bennett was among those who remained involved with the WILPF as individual members. What emerges from the extant records of her involvement in the WILPF from 1930 is an emphasis on international affairs, with little mention of events within the Irish branch. Most of her correspondence reflected her concern with the politics of China and India, particularly the issue of self-government for India. She consistently urged WILPF to debate and issue a statement on the latter issue, pointing out 'This is emphatically not a domestic problem. The W.I.L. action on it determines their point of view on Imperialism.' Her admiration of Gandhi is clear throughout this correspondence, and at one stage she hoped to travel to India as the WILPF representative at a women's congress in 1931 – a plan which was not realized. In addition it is clear that more and more of her time was spent attending international conferences, among them the world economic conference of the League of Nations, and conferences of the International Industrial Association. In 1928 she attended the League of Nations as a special representative of George Russell's journal, *The Irish Statesman*. In March 1931 she was appointed adviser to the Irish Labour delegation to the International Labour Organization conference in Geneva, a development she was particularly pleased with. Her correspondence with the WILPF fades out after 1933, by which time it had ceased to exist in Ireland, despite an attempt by Geneva to revive it in 1932. Bennett's personal commitment to pacifism never wavered, but increasingly from the 1920s her energies would be absorbed in her work within the trade union movement.

4

Trade unions and Irish women

Bennett cited the 1913 strike and lock-out in Dublin as a major influence in determining her future direction. Towards the end of her life she recalled her clandestine visits to Liberty Hall:

> At that time I belonged to the respectable middle class and I did not dare admit to my home circle that I had run with the crowd to hear Jim Larkin, and crept like a culprit into Liberty Hall to see Madame Markievicz in a big overall, with sleeves rolled up, presiding over a cauldron of stew, surrounded by a crowd of gaunt women and children carrying bowls and cans.[1]

Appalled at the condition of women and barefoot children she observed, Bennett undertook relief work to help strikers' families, but held back from direct involvement in Liberty Hall. She joined with other IWRL members in an aid scheme initiated by the Lady Mayoress, Mrs Sherlock, to provide daily meals for strikers' families. Appealing for support for the scheme which was endorsed by an *Irish Citizen* editorial, Bennett wrote, 'We are not all of one opinion as to whether workers or employers are in the right in this struggle: but none of us can witness misery unmoved, and misery abounds in Dublin just now.'[2] Relief work by this and other suffrage societies greatly strengthened bonds between the labour and suffrage movements. That such bonds endured is clear from a note in the *Workers' Republic* in 1915 that 'Several well known and experienced suffragists have kindly consented to undertake organising work in connection with the Union. They are women who showed us their sympathy two years ago.'[3] As yet Bennett was not included in this group. Immediately prior to the start of the strike in 1913, the findings of an IWRL investigation into working conditions for women in Dublin factories and shops were published in the *Irish Citizen*. Entitled 'Women's Work and Wages in Dublin', this series of articles included an examination of conditions within a number of firms which were in dispute with their female employees. The *Irish Citizen* welcomed the investigation, remarking:

> Let us set before our eyes and make known the actual state of things under which women in Ireland live, and we need no longer dread the reproach that the agitation in Ireland for woman suffrage is an alien importation.[4]

While accepting many common aims between the labour and women's movements, Bennett and other suffrage leaders continued to advise women groups to remain independent of any political alliance. Early in 1914 she pointed out that:

> A large number of the reforms we desire and hope to achieve by means of the vote are also the objective of the Labour Party. I am with those suffragists who believe they will find firm allies amongst the labour people. But that is not to advocate a union with the Labour Party. I do not think it would ever be advisable to form a union with any party. Suffragists must continue to take their own stand independent of any political party.[5]

That year there was disagreement at the Irish Trade Union Congress (ITUC) on whether a deputation from the IWRL should be admitted to speak on the issue of women's suffrage. The chairman, James Larkin, objected to such a deputation being received, principally because he believed one IWRL member to be against trade unions. Larkin argued that 'the suffrage could be used for or against their class'. William O'Brien and Tom Johnson pointed to the useful work done by the IWRL regarding meals for schoolchildren. James Connolly, while noting his preference for the militant wing of suffragism, argued that 'he was out to give women the vote, even if they used it against him as a human right'.[6] Bennett later recalled that Connolly had twice sought her involvement in trade union work.[7] Shortly before the 1916 Rising, her help was actively sought by Helena Molony in re-organizing the Irish Women Workers' Union (IWWU). Bennett later wondered why Molony had selected her for this work, commenting, 'I knew nothing about Trade Unionism, but I was drawn to Liberty Hall by the prickings of conscience so many of us felt after the 1913 strike.'[8] Bennett, although anxious to help, made it clear that she could not support any organization which threatened force. Connolly joined Molony and Bennett at this meeting, questioning Bennett's genuine commitment to helping women workers. Bennett later recalled having 'a warm discussion' with Connolly, challenging him as to the wisdom of bringing national politics into the Dublin labour movement.[9] She told Connolly plainly that she was a pacifist first and foremost and would not give up that principle for trade unionism. His response was that national freedom must come first.[10]

Writing to an American friend in the immediate aftermath of the 1916 Rising, Bennett included a lengthy impression of James Connolly, explaining that she was 'sure his name will be prominent as one of the leaders, if not the foremost leader of this business'. Her letter emphasizes that it was pacifist conviction that held her back from joining in his trade union work. She believed that Connolly disliked her, was opposed to her theories, and scorned anti-militancy in any form. However, while she and Connolly had disagreed publicly a number of times, she admired his intellect, noting:

> He was one of the best suffrage speakers I have ever heard and a thorough feminist in every respect: he taught the Transport Union of Dublin to support and respect the women workers' struggle for industrial and political rights.[11]

She described him as 'physically, intellectually and in character powerful to an exceptional degree. For me it was always an intellectual effort to follow him'. She believed that living and working conditions in Dublin allied to the treatment meted out to Connolly and the workers, had made him a bitter man, a fact she considered understandable, 'for he was shamefully and terribly treated'.[12] In an essay on Connolly and the Irish Rebellion written soon after the 1916 executions, Bennett described Connolly's death as the most irreparable loss to Ireland.

> A man of great intellect and powerful character, he might, had he devoted himself whole-heartedly to Labour, have revolutionized labour conditions in Dublin. [He] was a thinker with constructive ideas and organizing ability. His work for Labour was governed by his reason, and therefore valuable. Had he belonged to a nation other than Ireland he must have proved a prominent Labour leader. When the inner history of this rebellion becomes known, Connolly will surely stand out as the leading intellect in the plot.[13]

Citing Connolly's nationalism as an indestructible force, and echoing her ongoing efforts to gain independent recognition for Ireland within WILPF, she asked, 'How far is it immoral, even criminal to postpone practical recognition of the "sacred right of freedom" to this particular small nation of Ireland?' In her evidence to the American Commission five years later, Bennett stated:

> The manner of Connolly's death affected me very much personally, because I was in close touch with him. I knew his family, and I kept in touch with him when he was lying in prison, and of course at the time of his execution.[14]

Imprisoned after the Rising, Helena Molony made a further appeal to Bennett for help with the IWWU. Bennett obtained a visitor's permit for Mountjoy jail, where Molony implored her to help the women workers and revive their trade union. Bennett noted that Molony wanted her to do something for the women workers of Dublin, to 'see about getting a women's industry started – pottery, for instance, but for heaven's sake not shirtmaking!' This latter comment referred to a shirtmaking co-operative set up by Constance Markievicz and Helena Molony in Liberty Hall for women who were unemployed after the 1913 lockout. Many of these women were members of the Irish Citizen Army, and in the preparations for the 1916 Rising the women's co-operative became involved in the preparation of cartridges and bullets and various munition accessories.[15]

This time Bennett responded positively, and in August 1916 she and Helen Chenevix attended the Trade Union Congress in Sligo. Opinions differ as to whether she went at the invitation of Congress with a specific mandate to organize women workers. Bennett herself recalled that she had attended as an observer, 'not having then joined the movement'.[16] What is undisputed, however, is that from late 1916 she became identified with the work of the IWWU, an association which would continue for the next forty years. Bennett, Chenevix and Molony would form a formidable triumvirate on behalf of women workers. Describing this congress as the most inspiring she had ever attended, Bennett was particularly impressed by the presidential address of Tom Johnson. Johnson proposed the creation of a strong Irish Labour Party with a practical programme of social reconstruction, based on social justice and the political equality of all men and women. Bennett commented that:

> Johnson's opening address as chairman outlined a constructive programme for Ireland which was truly audacious in its hopefulness; it

> put courage and purposefulness into the heart of the congress. The Irish Labour movement was launched on a new road from that date.[17]

Certainly, she was on a new path from this time. Significantly, in the autumn of 1916, printed copies of Johnson's presidential address, 'The Future of Labour in Ireland', were included in a literature campaign by the IIL, being described as 'a really constructive contribution to the cause of social progress in Ireland'.

Outlining the process through which she became involved with the IWWU, Bennett viewed her attendance at the 1916 Irish Trade Union Congress and Labour Party (ITUCLP) as a first step in her trade union education. She recounted that Marion Duggan had in fact revived the IWWU in Liberty Hall before Bennett's involvement, but that Liberty Hall intimidated most women with what she termed 'its dour methods'. In addition, it was still physically in ruins and consequently uninviting. In January 1917 she was invited by the Liberty Hall group to organize 'the aristocrats of industry' – the women printers. Lent an office by the Typographical Society in Gardiner Street, she later recalled:

> I had absolutely no idea how to go about it. But I was burning with enthusiasm. I had no money. No office. No furniture. Nothing. But I went out and I got one member to start me off. I put her name down in a twopenny jotter and hoped fervently for more.[18]

Thus began what she described as a 'timid campaign' of waiting outside printers' workshops at six o'clock in the evening thrusting handbills upon uninterested women workers. The handbills invited them to meet at 35 Gardiner Street on Monday evenings, but initially there was little reaction. Bennett recalled that:

> Half a dozen or so of us waited in the long room lent to us for many a Monday evening before any interest in our effort was manifested. I felt rich when I carried home as many as thirty pennies in contributions. Then suddenly there came a stir and a rush: Monday evenings saw the long room packed with girls and women eager to pay their pennies and to pour their grievances into my confused ear.[19]

Soon women from other industries came to join. A bigger office was opened in Dame Street with a suffragist supporter supplying office furniture. Within months membership was over 2,000 and growing, and included women in the printing, box-making, laundry and textile industries. It was reported in the *Irish Citizen* that:

> The last six months has seen a growing sense of independence and of 'push' amongst the women workers . . . These women are going to prove themselves a new force in Irish affairs which no class of politicians can ignore.[20]

In the spring of 1918 the IWWU was officially registered as a trade union, with Bennett and Chenevix becoming honorary secretaries. By this time membership exceeded 5,000. From the outset Louie insisted that the union operate independently from Liberty Hall and remain solely a women's union, a point of much debate over the years. The union's first industrial action soon occurred. When the Dublin Master Printers' Association refused to recognize the IWWU and its pay claim on behalf of women printers, a six-week strike and lock-out ensued. Financial support from the Dublin Trades Council during the strike, and the subsequent successful outcome of the dispute gave a further boost to the unionization of women. The IWWU next sought to organize laundry workers. In September 1917 Bennett wrote to the owner of the Court Laundry, Cecil Watson, asking him to meet with her to discuss this issue. Watson indicated his support for unionization and improved wages, provided his competitors did likewise. Subsequently a meeting to organize his workers was held in the Court canteen.[21] Although they would have differences over the years, Watson would be one of Bennett's most supportive employers. In her study of the IWWU, Mary Jones has pointed out that from this time the union actively sought the co-operation of employers in favouring trade union labour. In negotiations with employers, Bennett's policy would be conciliatory rather than confrontational. In December 1917 she assured the proprietors of the Lucan Woollen Mills that in return for their co-operation in favouring union labour, the IWWU would:

> Make every reasonable effort to cooperate with you in securing good work from your employees. We desire to have it understood that it is not our wish or purpose as a trade union to set ourselves in opposition to the employers.[22]

In 1922 Bennett commented that given good conditions and a little consideration, women workers would show loyalty towards a good employer, although she conceded that such employers were rare. Preference for conciliation, however, did not mean a lack of commitment to strong action by the union on behalf of its members, as subsequent strike action would demonstrate. From the beginning, union policy concentrated as much on improving working conditions as on wage increases. Bennett maintained that whereas wages were the primary concern of male workers, for women workers conditions were equally important. Describing current industrial practices as soul-destroying, she argued that women sought to bring the *humanities* into industrial life, declaring 'Holidays, shorter hours, and a little latitude as to spells of leisure during working hours, are concessions dear to women in factories or workshops.'[23] Recalling the laughter and wild exultation which had greeted union assertions in 1917 of a worker's right to one week of paid summer holiday – an unheard of proposition then – she noted that this gain was far more appreciated by women than a wage increase. Her concern with working conditions concentrated much on health and safety in the workplace. She pointed to apathy on the part of both employers and trade unionists in this regard, noting that even the very minimal standards then set down by the Factory Acts were rarely attained. In particular she argued for more women factory inspectors, pointing out that the Free State government had appointed a total of four factory inspectors for the whole country, only one of whom was female. Insistence on a humanizing element in industry would, she argued, have beneficial effects both on the health and happiness of workers and on the success of industry itself. She demanded on behalf of the IWWU and the Irish Labour Women's Council a standard by which human values would gain precedence over industrial value – 'Efficiency and prosperity bought with the soul of the worker must generate ultimately a poisonous element in the social system.' The following year, in the same vein, she argued that workers' desire for control over industries derived not from an acquisitive instinct, but from a reaction to industrialism:

> The urge of growth, physical and spiritual, is forcing men and women in factory and workshop to rebellion against conditions which cramp and cripple human development. This is an urge so fundamental that it cannot be finally denied or repressed: it must ultimately sweep away all the restraints which the capitalistic system may impose upon it.[24]

Bennett observed that the spirit of self-sacrifice among the strikers in refusing proffered increases without union recognition was crucial. She registered what would be a recurring theme of hers over the years – that the religious spirit of women was a significant factor in the loyalty of Irish women workers. She felt that, perhaps, the insistence of

Catholicism on loyalty probably strengthened this instinct among members, but that also religion had helped somewhat to redeem the trade unionism of Irish women 'from the sordid and mercenary atmosphere which haunts trade unionism in general'.[25] Her subsequent trade union career reflected her revulsion from what she saw as the 'sordid and mercenary'. Her attitude was one of conciliation and compromise.

Under the aegis of the IWWU, the Irish Nurses' Union (INU) was established in 1919, one of the first of its kind in Europe. The *Irish Times*' sense of horror at this development showed the depth of opposition existing toward women's organizations. Nurses were asked 'not to dethrone and degrade the profession by dallying with the promises of Trade Unionism. A strike of nurses would be hardly less painful and disconcerting than a strike of wives in favour of, say, a forty-hour week of domestic activity.'[26] Helena Molony proceeded to shock that paper even further by establishing a Domestic Workers' Union. Allied to this was a proposal for an employment bureau for domestic workers. Both ventures were unsuccessful. Molony attempted to unionize this section of workers a number of times over the coming years, but with no great degree of success.

Not surprisingly Bennett's intense involvement in the IWWU was reflected in the pages of the *Irish Citizen* during her periods of editorship. Increasingly, articles and editorials focused on the pay and conditions of women workers. Trade unionists had anticipated post-war problems arising from lower wages paid to women workers who had been drafted in to fill men's jobs. In this regard Bennett wrote that the demand for equal pay for equal work should have been maintained by suffrage societies.[27] During the war years, women's pay – whether in regular industry or in specific war-related industries – was a particular bone of contention. Distress among women workers had been dismissed in the House of Commons because 'Most women workers have men in their families or are getting separation allowances.'[28] Bennett's front-page editorial in December 1916 responded that, 'It is important for the whole future of the Labour movement that women should now maintain their claim for a Fair Living Wage, quite apart from any consideration of their family circumstances.' This was in keeping with a resolution recently passed by the IWSF executive in protest against low wages paid for munitions work to women of comfortable means. An editorial by Bennett in the *Irish Citizen* encompassed her main concerns:

> The enormous extension of women's employment owing to the war has not helped to promote the real independence of women. They are in the

> majority of cases paid far less than the men they have replaced. It is a plain fact that the whole government of the country is controlled by the male intelligence. We have always maintained that this is inevitable in a militarist state.[29]

During the summer of 1917 the *Irish Citizen* editorial noted the establishment of communal kitchens in Dublin, serving meals at cost-price. Six such centres existed, including one at Liberty Hall. The *Irish Citizen* encouraged such developments, urging the establishment of a working women's restaurant wherein a good meal at moderate charge would be available each day. Other issues given prominence were the need for improved housing, municipal nurseries and playgrounds. Such policies strongly reflected the thinking of Bennett, Chenevix and the IWRL. In an essay on Bennett, Ellen Hazelkorn has noted the repeated calls in the *Irish Citizen* of this period for women workers to 'organise, organise', one issue announcing the emergence of a class hitherto unheard of – the woman worker – 'aroused at last to a realisation that her fate is in her own hands and that she has in trade unionism a force to control it'.[30] Bennett's close identification with Labour did not inhibit criticism where she felt it necessary. During the Irish Convention of 1917, the *Irish Citizen* reported:

> When Labour Sunday was celebrated in Dublin a few weeks ago, no woman was invited to stand on the platform by the Labour Party. The women of Ireland might have all been free to enjoy the comforts of a home, a fireside, and a cradle to rock for all the interest the Labour Party of Ireland manifested in their affairs.[31]

Similarly in 1918, Bennett recorded the great disappointment felt by the IWWU that no reference had been made at the All-Ireland Conference to the part played by women in the campaign against conscription. By 1920, the *Irish Citizen* was devoting a special page to women workers 'in accordance with the policy of feminism, peace and labour for which it had always stood'. This page detailed the activities of the women's unions, strikes, pay claims and branch affairs. Eventually the IWWU and the INU decided to use the paper as their official journal and source of communication with members throughout the country. Nurses were asked to read every line and discuss topics at their branch meetings. This interaction of the suffrage and labour movements produced new bonds and inevitably new demands for radical approaches on the women's question. The IWWU appealed to readers of the *Irish Citizen* to influence women workers to join the union. To mark Saint Brigid's day 1920, the IWWU held a conference in Dublin's Mansion House, deemed 'a Parliament of Working Women', and Brigid was chosen as the patron saint of the union. The union retained its commitment to Saint Brigid over the years. Saint Brigid was also the name chosen by Bennett in 1930 for her new home in Killiney.

In November 1919 Bennett initiated a debate in the *Irish Citizen* on the issue of separate trade unions for women. A lively exchange took place between her and Cissie Cahalan (Irish Linen Drapers' Assistants' Association) on this option versus the 'one big union' concept. Advocating separate organization, Bennett argued that equality of opportunity for women and men in industry was far from established. In addition to the matter of unequal pay, she pointed out that women were excluded from certain industries. Declaring that it was futile to deny latent antagonism between the sexes in industry, Bennett argued:

> There has been too facile an acceptance of the theory that women and men are best organised in the same Trade Union. Woman's instinct drives her most often to a purely feminine organisation. There is a disposition amongst men workers not only to keep women in inferior and subordinate positions, but to drive them out of industry altogether. Moreover, men have not the same aspirations for women as women have for themselves, and in a mixed organisation much time and trouble would have to be wasted in securing the co-operation of men in a demand for reforms of which women may feel urgent need.[32]

Pointing out that within mixed trade unions men were almost always dominant, she commented that, 'So long as women occupy a subordinate position within the Trade Union movement they will need the safeguard of an independent organisation'. In addition she noted that pay increases demanded and accepted for women workers within mixed unions were almost always considerably less than those obtained for men. She believed that the opposite should be the case because of the notoriously low wages historically applying to women's work. Rather than the 'one big union' concept, Bennett advocated an Irish Women Workers' Federation 'strong enough to serve as a force in raising the status of women in industry, and in influencing public opinion on industrial and social problems where they particularly affect women'. Such a federation should co-operate closely with male unions on matters of common interest. In addition to the issue of pay, Bennett highlighted other areas needing consideration:

> The question of the hours of women's work, of night work, and of work before and after child-birth, are all being debated at the present time, and

> all are questions which women workers themselves should consider and decide upon. How can they do so if they have not an organisation through which to express their particular point of view?[33]

Cissie Cahalan, one of the few working-class women involved in the Irish suffrage movement, defended the concept of mixed trade unions. She laid the blame for the under-involvement of women on their own shoulders, arguing that women's reluctance to go forward as candidates for branch or executive committees left the management of trade unions in male hands. Claiming that Bennett was, in fact, advocating the perpetuation of sex antagonism, she argued that while the position of women in the labour movement was weak, it was not subordinate, and could become stronger if women ceased to be apathetic and took up their responsibilities. She claimed further that gender-segregated unions might prove an effective weapon for bosses in times of dispute, arguing:

> I would remind Miss Bennett that the pioneers of the Suffrage did not seek to establish a separate parliament for women, but demanded a place in the nation's parliament. If women in the industrial world want a place in the labour movement, they must seek it in the Labour Parliament, shoulder to shoulder with the men and not in any separate organisation apart and isolated.[34]

While Bennett agreed that women had been apathetic, she argued that male-managed trade unions were not the answer. Instead she urged that women be educated in union affairs and have responsibility thrust upon them. When women learned to manage their own affairs, they would then have the confidence to participate in mixed unions and trade councils on an equal footing with men. The debate continued for many years, Bennett's involvement within the trade union movement reinforcing her beliefs. In 1922 she declared that:

> The feminist movement never touched Irish industrial workers, therefore the same old attitude of male superiority persists, and women in industry are assigned (and for the most part accept without protest) an inferior position not only in the workshops but in the Trade Unions. It is only in a women's organisation, controlled altogether by women, that it is possible to appreciate the existence of an outlook upon industrial problems which may be called distinctly feminine.[35]

In 1930 Bennett was still arguing the need for a separate women's union. Commenting that but for the IWWU, women's voices were rarely heard at trades union congress or trades council, she pointed to areas of women's employment – teachers, clerical workers, shop assistants – which were almost always represented by men. She commented wryly, 'What a touching and flattering confidence in the male sex.'[36] Interestingly, her critic from 1919, Cissie Cahalan, writing in the same issue of the journal, observed that it was 'deplorable to find men who still think of woman as the enemy – and shut their eyes to the real barrier to a full and complete life for all – the capitalist class'.[37] Helena Molony likewise concluded that working women had made little progress since Connolly's time, pointing out that women were still excluded from certain industries because of their gender, and that a woman's wage was still only twenty to thirty per cent of a man's average wage.[38]

While disagreement with Bennett's views concentrated mainly on the issue of single-sex unions, little criticism was voiced towards her views regarding women's right to work. Her key role as Secretary of the IWWU should have placed her in a strong position to demand equality of opportunity for women in all areas of work. In the 'equal pay for equal work' scenario, debate had concentrated on the issue of pay. Bennett believed that the real problem lay in the issue of equal work. She did not believe the time was right for women to 'invade' men's industrial preserves, claiming that, 'the class war must be fought out before women could fight for equality of opportunity'. Referring, in 1919, to the controversial question of women's admittance to skilled trades she explained:

> The struggle for equality of opportunity in professions seems to be approaching universal success, but it has only begun in industry. And in industry the position is much more difficult and complicated for many reasons. The entry of women into skilled trades even on the same terms as men must inevitably mean some disemployment for men; and the fact that the majority of working men are the supporters of a wife and children and only a minority of working women have similar responsibilities, makes the most progressive of us hesitate to urge women industrial workers to invade men's trades.

Noting that already in post-war England there was considerable antagonism towards women in the labour movement, Bennett commented that:

> The 'class war' must be fought out, and the present industrial system revolutionised before women workers can, with just consideration for wives and mothers, make any real fight for equality of opportunity. In a

> society where the financial burden of keeping the home lies upon the male wage-earner, working under a system so heedless of human needs as the industrial system of today, it would be madness for women workers to attempt to disturb fundamentally the present distribution of industrial work.[39]

Bennett argued that equality of opportunity could only be achieved when co-operation replaced capitalism, and that it was woman's task to lead in this development. In the meantime a woman's organization could do much to raise the general status of women in industry. Bennett's views were reinforced over the following years when deteriorating employment opportunities in Ireland became allied to an increased perception of the woman worker as a threat.

Bennett's public career commenced at a time of intense political activity in the country. Throughout that career she retained a keen interest in political matters and did not hesitate to make her views known within both trade union and Labour Party circles. In January 1918 the Representation of the People Act granted the parliamentary vote to women over thirty who were graduates or property holders. The vote was also extended to men of twenty one years. The age provision avoided the immediate establishment of a female majority in the electorate. While the *Irish Citizen* rejoiced that the sex barrier had at last been broken, it called for the removal of the age restriction, and advised suffragists to work for votes for all women. Despite its limitations, the extension of the franchise created demands for greater female involvement in national affairs.[40] Bennett was the first woman candidate nominated to stand for the 1918 general election. The *Irish Citizen* congratulated the Irish Labour Party on being the first political party to choose a woman candidate. Bennett subsequently declined the invitation due, no doubt, to the intense machinations between Labour and Sinn Féin as to whether or not Labour should contest the election. Ultimately Labour succumbed to Sinn Féin pressure and withdrew from the election. In addition to ideological differences between the two parties, Sinn Féin feared that Labour's participation would prevent its outright victory over the Irish Parliamentary Party.[41] Michael Laffan has pointed out that while Tom Johnson claimed Labour had been the only party prepared to sacrifice itself in the interests of the nation, the reality was that large numbers of Labour supporters had declared they would vote Sinn Féin.[42] No contemporary record survives of Bennett's reaction to this development, although she later wrote that it had been Labour Party policy to remain apart from Sinn Féin for the sake of social and economic policy.[43] Possibly, she also felt that her primary commitment at this stage was to the development of the IWWU. In fact it was a Sinn Féin candidate – Constance Markievicz – who achieved at this election the distinction of being the first woman elected to the House of Commons.

The ITUC congress of 1918 discussed the implications of the new women voters. William O'Brien noted that 'means must now be found to associate them with us in our political as well as in our industrial work'.[44] However, reporting on the local elections of the following year, Hanna Sheehy Skeffington noted that 'official labour has the unenviable distinction of entirely ignoring women on their ticket'.[45] The question of direct political involvement by the IWWU was to be a source of disagreement within the union over the next two decades. Rank and file members consistently opposed the establishment of a political fund or affiliation to any political party. On one occasion in 1924 the union executive sought a specific mandate to establish a political fund aimed at the election of women to local government and public boards. This was refused by delegates.[46] The possible divisiveness of political differences, particularly on the issue of the recognition of the Free State government, added to a belief that the IWWU should focus on industrial matters alone. The attitude of the Labour Party did little to encourage change. Describing overtures made to the party from the IWWU in 1923, Jones has noted that 'articulate women trade unionists found only a measured welcome'.[47] Following Labour's rebuff, Bennett established a sub-committee within the IWWU to deal with 'social, civic and educational matters'. This would act in unison with, but be independent of, the Women's Labour Council.[48] Generally during Bennett's early years with the union, particularly spanning the Anglo-Irish and civil wars, official comment on topical issues was restricted to humanitarian and economic matters. Arthur Mitchell has noted that civil war differences ensured that political and constitutional issues continued to dominate Irish life throughout the 1920s, to the disadvantage of Labour. He also notes that the election of seventeen Labour party candidates in 1922 was partly due to their emphasis on social and economic concerns, and partly due to the wish of many voters to avoid the treaty issue.[49]

From the formation of the Labour Party in 1912 until 1930, both the political and industrial branches of the movement were contained in one organization, the party congress. Unique among European labour movements at this time, Irish labour leaders believed that this combination of functions provided greater security, particularly given the unsettled conditions in Ireland. The only demand for a separation of these functions during the 1920s came from the IWWU. At every party conference from 1924 Bennett and her executive urged the separation of the two arms of the movement.[50] Following Labour's success in the 1922 election, Bennett wrote that the Irish Labour Party now had a great opportunity to draw people towards a conception of liberty as envisaged by the men of 1916. Referring to what she termed 'the death-agonies of the Republican Party that was once the nation's idol', she appealed to labour leaders to be bold in defining their ultimate goal, and win the allegiance of workers with a republican bias. The co-operation of women workers, she observed, would be crucial to Labour's success in this area. She advocated two wings for the party, an industrial wing and a parliamentary wing. Insisting that the industrial wing be distinct from the parliamentary, she argued:

> Thus far, Labour in the Dáil has shown itself definitely reformist rather than revolutionary. Irish Labour must develop a constructive industrial and agricultural policy of its own . . . a policy which can be initiated without unending appeals to the Government. Labour must become self-reliant . . . Too much concentration on political affairs will impede such a development.[51]

Observing that the real force of a labour movement lay in the rank and file, Bennett declared that a parliamentary labour party would be worse than useless if not backed by a progressive public spirit from the trade unions. Accepting the lack of vision shown by Labour leaders, with little effort made to instruct the rank and file in new opportunities, she argued:

> Every Trade Unionist here should know that an independent Irish Republic is only attainable through those democratic principles which are the pillars of Labour all over the world, and that a Republic not founded upon these is of no more value to us workers than British or Free State rule.

Referring to feminism and the organization of women in Ireland, Bennett stated:

> Trade Unionism amongst our women is a thing of recent growth – so recent that women of the working class are almost a dumb factor in our nation's life. The Irish Women Workers' Union is the only body which expresses the views of Irish working women. But women Trade

> Unionists have not sufficient influence to push through any policy; as yet they can only suggest and nag.[52]

Referring to the quite different patterns of the Irish and English suffrage movements, Bennett observed that the 'desire for enfranchisement has never played a vital part in our political history. So Feminism awoke to the call of militarism, instead of to reform.' Recalling Frank Sheehy Skeffington's mockery of Cumann na mBan for its subservient role to the Volunteers, she noted that in Ireland, as elsewhere, 'women are the victims of the intellectual indolence bred in them for centuries. They have used emancipation to follow on the heels of men, without asking whither or why.' Accepting that currently Cumann na mBan had drawn to itself most of the intelligent and high-spirited working-class women, she argued that it was purely a fighting force, with no constructive ideals for nation or class. Echoing reservations made earlier in 1922 to Emily Balch, Bennett commented:

> There was much that was admirable, much detestable, and much that was pitiful in the attitude of Republican women towards the recent civil strife in Ireland. They failed in sane, constructive thinking. Their ignorance of affairs outside Ireland is as unfortunate as their failure to appreciate the value of cultural and social influences. If Labour came forward now with an appeal to every worker to join in a campaign of education and of economic and social enterprises directed towards the development of an independent Co-operative Commonwealth, the women workers now absorbed by Cumann na mBan would quickly rally in support of this better way to freedom. They would recognise that the time had come to stack the guns and take to the plough and the shuttle for Ireland's sake. Where the women go, the men will follow.[53]

As outlined in Chapter 3, Bennett's criticism of what she saw as the tunnel vision of republican women would continue to cause reverberations within the pacifist movement in Ireland.

It is clear that from 1918 onwards Bennett was held in high regard by politicians and employers, despite differing ideals and priorities. During the 1920s and 30s her name occurs regularly on a variety of committees and commissions, some related to labour issues, others to do with the international recognition of the Irish state. Her wide-ranging contacts at home and abroad made her a very useful emissary. Early in 1921, at the request of the Minister for Labour, she agreed to serve on a Dáil commission to formulate 'A Labour Policy for the Irish State'.[54] Following a number of seizures by workers of their factories during

1921, Bennett and Molony urged the Labour Party to produce a strategy 'to help other bodies of workers to conduct industries which they might have to take over'.[55] In addition to attending executive meetings of WILPF during the 1920s, Bennett frequently attended League of Nations economic conferences in Geneva. She attended one such conference as a representative of *The Irish Statesman*, the weekly journal edited by George Russell.[56] Rising unemployment during the 1920s, aggravated by increased mechanization and work-measurement schemes, prompted IWWU initiatives on behalf of the unemployed. A campaign was launched in 1925 seeking the extension of unemployment benefits. Deputations to this effect were issued to Dáil, Senate, poor law and civic commissioners. The government response to such demands was harsh. Joe Lee has noted that during the 1920s the Cabinet waged a coherent campaign against the weaker elements in the community, taking the view that the poor were responsible for their poverty. Unemployment was deemed to be the result of either laziness on the part of the unemployed or the restrictive practices of trade unions. Lee also notes that W.T. Cosgrave institutionalized the neglect of labour by demoting the Department of Labour, established by the first Dáil, to a mere section of the Department of Industry and Finance.[57]

Announcing the cessation of certain unemployment payments in 1924, the Minister for Industry and Finance, Patrick McGilligan, stated that the government had no responsibility to provide work.[58] This was the background against which Bennett and the IWWU operated. In 1926 Bennett wrote to President Cosgrave protesting against government action to relieve distress in Dublin by distributing food tickets from the Dublin union [workhouse] rather than from unemployment exchanges. Over the years Bennett insisted that due regard be made for the dignity of those in receipt of any such relief. A committee for the relief of unemployment, established in 1927, included representation from all political parties, but President Cosgrave refused to appoint a woman member. Its subsequent report in 1928 contained no reference to women. The IWWU was particularly critical of Labour members of this committee who had, in effect, ignored women workers and would doubtless have agreed with Jones' comment that 'quite clearly, the question of the employment of women had no place on the political agenda'.[59] Nor would it appear that outside the IWWU executive political concerns were very high on the agenda of ordinary union members. Apart from pay – and work-related issues, members' main interests focused on the union's extensive social activities. Allied to the continued rejection of its attempts to establish a political wing, the frustration and impatience of the IWWU executive can be judged in its criticism of poor member participation in the May Day celebrations of 1929:

> So far as women are concerned, the May Day demonstration organised by the Dublin Trade Union Council last year demonstrated only that Dublin women are too shy, too proud, too indolent or too stupid to support the men trade unionists in a triumphant display of solidarity.[60]

Writing in the *Dublin Labour Year Book of 1930*, Bennett, Molony and Cahalan each addressed the issue of women in the political wing of labour. All were unhappy with that role. Molony, referring to the 'sorry travesty of emancipation', advised women and the labour movement to reflect on Connolly's writings and beliefs. Bennett noted that, despite the fact that women made up fifty per cent of the electorate, political parties still treated them as a side issue, and women themselves made little use of their political power. She commented that politically the labour movement was completely in the hands of men, and it was evident that working-class women did not desire to be so involved. In a similar vein, Cahalan noted that there was not one woman labour representative in the Dáil or Senate. She observed that this reflected the situation of women within the labour movement itself, pointing to the few women delegates appointed to the male-dominated Irish Labour Party and Trade Union Congress (ILPTUC).

In 1932 Bennett became the first woman president of the Irish Trade Union Congress. While there was some criticism of the fact that she was a president who was not working-class, Bennett's commitment, as Jones has pointed out, to placing the needs of working women on the agenda was beyond dispute. Her address to the congress reflected her international and trade union concerns, particularly in relation to the growing threat of fascism. Warning of the danger for workers and trade unionism through government power over industry under the capitalist system, Bennett commented that the fascist tendencies in this regard of both governments the Saorstat had experienced was a cause for concern.[61] Forecasting rapid revolutionary changes in the economic structure of many countries, including Ireland, she urged the trade union movement to cease using defensive tactics. Instead she advocated a bold campaign for the acquisition of power to control the new situation, declaring that, 'control must be the slogan of Trade Unionism. Control starting from the workshop with Works' Councils, carried on to industries through the trade unions and to economic life through a

National Economic Council'.[62] In the light of increased mechanization allied to increased unemployment and lower wage rates being paid to women workers, she outlined two strategies that trade unionism could pursue. She advocated the adoption of a wage scale based on standards of living rather than on skill or education. She also insisted that trade unions should adopt the same pay scale for men and women in industry; claim, for all workers, a wage adequate to support dependants; and oppose the concept that simplified mechanical processes necessarily involved the use of cheap labour. These aims she acknowledged would be unpopular.

During the 1920s further attempts had been made by Bennett and the IWWU executive to persuade members to establish a political wing, but to no avail. With the voluntary separation of the political and industrial branches of Labour in 1930, Bennett again urged women to enter the political arena. Conceding that there was little evidence of effort by the Labour Party to win the confidence of working women, she nonetheless urged women to become involved. Cautioning members that old prejudices still existed, and that women should be wary of accepting a powerless role within the Party, she urged women to remember that 'the movement is bigger than any of us, bigger than any section of us. We women have our part to play in it, and if the men fail to open the doors for our entry, then we must open them for ourselves.'[63] The way to open doors, she argued, was to form a political wing. If members agreed to this she promised that the IWWU would demand a share in leadership and policy decisions. Towards the end of 1933, members finally agreed to the formation of a political wing of the IWWU, prompted no doubt by moves that had been developing since the late 1920s to restrict women's employment.

The trade union movement generally supported restrictions on women workers, viewing their lower wage rates as a threat to male workers at a time of high unemployment. From 1934 attention focused on Sean Lemass's forthcoming Bill on conditions of employment. The IWWU sought and was refused consultative status in the framing of this Bill.[64] Lemass agreed to receive its deputation only when the final draft was ready. The powerlessness of the IWWU was emphasized when the government enforced an old Act making mandatory throughout industry a holiday for women and juveniles when St Patrick's Day fell on a Sunday.[65] Such a selective legislative move did not bode well for the forthcoming Bill. At their 1935 annual convention, IWWU delegates voted in favour of affiliation to the Irish Labour Party and indicated their intention to resist all attempts to restrict women's employment. Bennett took a high-profile stance in this campaign. Replying to one critic who argued man's right to be the protector and breadwinner, she asked what man would fulfill this role for elderly spinsters or widows with unmarried daughters. Similarly, she asked, was a father on low income to provide for adult daughters? If such benefits were to be state funded, were men prepared for extra taxation? Declaring that women were necessary and not superfluous workers she argued that their inferior political status had until recently contributed to their exploitation as workers. Employers, male fellow workers and government had all assisted in that exploitation. Regarding government attempts to cope with unemployment by replacing women workers with men, she asked if hunger and want were more tolerable to women than men. She did not accept that Lemass's proposals to restrict women's employment addressed the fundamental problem of unemployment, arguing that they in fact posed a threat to all workers. For Bennett, the only sound policy was one of equal status for all workers, a wage scale based on the value of work without sex discrimination, and shorter working hours. This trenchant defence of women's right to work was modified somewhat by her concession that women were more suited to certain industries than men, for example, the textile, sugar, confectionery and tobacco industries. She also made the amazing statement that, 'there are many mechanical processes so monotonous that men find them intolerable. Women endure such monotony with less evil effect on their nervous system'.[66]

Over the summer of 1935, the battle over the Conditions of Employment Act was at its height. While assuring the IWWU that the status of women workers would not be affected, Lemass refused to delete Section 12 which gave the government power to restrict or prohibit the employment of women in industry. In the Dáil debate on the Bill Lemass argued against the objections put forward by Bennett and the IWWU. He did, however, agree on some points with Bennett, conceding her point that, as a result of mechanization, women were now doing in the factory work that they had previously done at home, and could not be dismissed as superfluous workers.[67] Following his announcement that deputations would be received from interested parties regarding amendments to the Bill, the IWWU looked to the Labour Party for support, but to no avail. In May 1935 the IWWU executive had expressed its concern that some male trade unionists shared the government's point of view regarding the displacement of women from industry by men.[68]

Subsequently, at a meeting with the party leader, William Norton, it became clear that no support would be forthcoming for the women's stance. In fact, Norton told a Labour Party conference that Congress welcomed the Bill as a safeguard against exploiting employers.[69] In protest, Bennett was authorized by her executive to withhold affiliation fees to the Party until further notice. The long argued for alliance with Labour had lasted less than two years.

The IWWU started a press and leaflet campaign outlining the implications of Section 12 and seeking the support of male trade unionists. Debate on the issue at the ITUC in August 1935 showed the extent of trade union hostility to any amendment. Proposing a motion on 'equal rights and equal pay' on behalf of the IWWU, Bennett moved that, 'This Congress reaffirms its allegiance to the fundamental principle of equal rights and equal democratic opportunities for all citizens and equal pay for equal work.'[70] Pointing out that the restrictive powers of the proposed Act were merely a prelude to other legislative developments which could impose a dangerous form of control on all workers, she argued that the question was not one of sex but of wages, and should be dealt with as such. She noted that the IWWU saw plainly in the Bill a fascist tendency to cripple the powers already held by trade unions.[71] William O'Brien of the Irish Transport and General Workers' Union (ITGWU), while seconding the resolution, offered his union's support for Section 12 which, he revealed, had been framed in response to a request from his national executive. In the ensuing debate, the replacement of male workers by lower-paid female workers was argued by most speakers as justification that men should benefit under the Act.[72] Generally it was felt to be 'a very wrong thing that young girls should be sent into factories and young men kept out'. Some women trade unionists, especially those from mixed unions, supported this stance, commenting that 'too many women inside the factory were a menace to the industrial classes'. The congress secretary argued that while the labour movement generally was in favour of equality, increasing mechanization, which favoured the replacement of male workers with cheaper female workers, posed a dilemma. He, along with the majority of members, believed that the needs of male workers should be paramount to preserve the greater good of working people generally. Defending the right of man as breadwinner, one speaker enthusiastically declared, 'Woman is the queen of our hearts and of our homes, and for God's sake let us try to keep her there.' Helena Molony in a scathing reply declared that it was 'terrible to find such reactionary opinions expressed . . . by responsible leaders of

Labour in support of a capitalist Minister in setting up a barrier against one set of citizens'.[73] William Norton, was adamant in his opposition to the IWWU, citing Molony's assertion of women's right to be carpenters and blacksmiths as proof of a wish by women workers to displace men. In addition he ordered a public reading of the memorandum presented to Lemass by congress which, he claimed, committed congress in principle to the restriction of women in the workplace. In concluding the case for women workers, Bennett asked, 'were the delegates going to give the Government power to deal with one section of the community as they liked?'

The final insult to the IWWU was the passing by congress of the resolution on equality of rights and pay.[74] The IWWU stance was supported by women's groups at home and abroad. Early in 1935 a conference of all women's organizations held by the IWWU in Dublin had protested to the government about the proposed restrictions on women's work. A memorandum issued by Bennett on behalf of this conference pointed out that whereas before 1916 women in Ireland held an inferior position, it was anticipated that the establishment of an Irish government would ensure female equality with men:

> In certain matters such as the citizenship laws, [women's] hopes have been justified, but more recent legislation shows a violent movement in the opposite direction, depriving women of fundamental liberties, and suggesting that the Government is permitting itself to be influenced by the incentive which is overthrowing democratic freedom and establishing bureaucratic dictatorships in certain European states.[75]

Other areas of concern to women's groups in Ireland were raised in this memorandum – a copy of which was sent by Bennett to President de Valera. These included various legislative discriminations affecting women, such as: the issue of nationality being recognized only through the father; non-compulsory jury service for women, resulting in women litigants almost always facing all-male juries; a ban on married women in the civil service, including widows; and differential salary scales for men and women teachers. In response to Bennett's request, de Valera met a deputation from the group to discuss the status of women in the Free State. She subsequently reported to the IWWU executive the delegation's disappointment that the president 'could not see how men and women could be equal', and that he seemed to know very little about the pending Employment Bill.[76]

Associated women's groups throughout the world were kept informed of developments through the pages of *The International Women's News*, a continuation of the former suffrage paper *Jus Suffragii*. During the 1930s details were published of Free State legislation affecting the status and equality of women, including much detail on industrial legislation. This period saw intense debate in women's journals worldwide on the issues of women's right to work, to retain their nationality after marriage, and their relegation to the domestic sphere under fascist regimes. With the establishment by the League of Nations of an inquiry into the civil and political status of women in 1935, a meeting was held in Dublin's Mansion House at which many well-known women voiced their opposition to the Conditions of Employment Bill. Speakers included Professor Mary Hayden, Hanna Sheehy Skeffington and Dorothy McArdle (the latter a staunch supporter of de Valera). At this meeting, Bennett restated her view that Lemass's concern was not for the welfare of women but for their control. She further stated that the Labour Party had not faced the question of arbitrary limitation of female employment squarely:

> The Minister for Industry and Commerce had faced the question: he knew what he wanted, and was building up a departmental control of all the country's industries. The Conditions of Employment Bill was a sugar-coated pill for the workers. It was a long step towards the Corporate State.[77]

Shades of suffrage activism emerged with the formation of a standing committee representing various women's organizations. In co-operation with the IWWU, this committee, of which Bennett was chair, initiated a publicity campaign to oppose the Bill and inform the public of its implications. There was support also in the Senate where the Bill was strongly attacked by Kathleen Clarke and Jennie Wyse Power. Clarke argued that the Bill contradicted the equality of citizens declared in the 1916 Proclamation, noting that some justification might have been acceptable if certain industries were deemed injurious to women's health, rather than the apparent blatant attempt to exclude women from the workforce. Clarke declared, 'I would be perfectly in agreement if he said I am going to prevent women from ever scrubbing floors and I will make men do it instead . . . Scrubbing floors is an ugly, hard and badly paid job, and men do not want it.'[78] Jennie Wyse Power, another Fianna Fáil senator, pointed out the importance of women's wages for family support, stating angrily that women did not want groups of men deciding these issues. In effect, however, that is precisely what happened.

Despite leaflet campaigns, street demonstrations, and the intensive lobbying of politicians and the public, Lemass dismissed women's protests as completely unrepresentative of the vast majority of women. The Bill became law in 1936, with majority support in both houses of the Oireachtas, including all Labour representatives.[79]

While it has been argued that the practical effects of the 1936 Bill on women's employment was negligible,[80] the psychological effects cannot be underestimated, and were embellished by the constitution of 1937. Bennett and the IWWU joined other women's groups in protest against certain articles relating to women within the proposed constitution. As Margaret Ward has noted, women's groups were unanimous in denouncing the omission of any statement regarding women's rights and opportunities as sinister and retrogressive.[81] A copy of Bennett's letter to President de Valera in May 1937 regarding sections in the constitution relating to women gained much publicity in the *Irish Press*. Here Bennett stated that 'certain sections are dangerous not so much for what they actually state as because of their ambiguity and the implications that may be given to them'. In particular she pointed out that the IWWU objected to Articles 40, 41 and 45. The latter she argued was the most indefensible from a woman's point of view as 'it takes from women the right to choose their own avocation in life. The State is given power to decide what avocations are suited to their sex and strength.' Bennett questioned who would decide the avocations deemed suitable to women. Article 40.1, which gave the state power to restrict the rights and liberties of certain citizens depending on differences of physical and moral capacity, and of social function, was criticized for placing women in a different category of citizenship to that of men. She described this clause as 'an invitation to anti-feminist prejudice'. Further, she argued that the vagueness of the clause left it open to interpretation against a social class or other group which, in a period of fascist ideology, was to be viewed with suspicion. The phrase 'due regard to differences of social function' Bennett claimed very definitely implied inequalities before the law. Regarding Article 41.2.1 she suggested an amendment to the restrictive phrase describing state recognition of woman's life '*within* the home', to one which recognized woman's 'work *for* the home'. Such an amendment, Bennett claimed, would give recognition to the value of work carried out in the interests of the home and the family by those women in public life who were not all mothers, but who had the specialized knowledge necessary for legislative changes in these areas. Regarding Article 41.2.2 she stated succinctly that a just distribution of wealth would render this article superfluous, commenting that the abolition of poverty and unemployment would make the need to 'protect' mothers unnecessary.[82] In her private notes Bennett indicated that:

> A counter balancing safeguard [is] required. All these clauses taken together will encourage a tendency to discriminate in legislation on grounds of sex. A clause [is needed] to ensure that neither in matters of employment and remuneration nor in opportunities to enter professions and public services should there be discrimination against any citizen on the sole ground of sex.[83]

Again, a dichotomy emerges in her arguments. While viewing Article 41 as a danger to the employment of married women she suggests, at the same time, that 'government policy should be [to ensure] a wage standard sufficient to maintain wife and family in frugal comfort'.[84] This displayed an attitude not totally removed from that of de Valera, who introduced the constitution to the Dáil by declaring that the breadwinner, 'who is normally and naturally the father of the family . . . should have sufficient income to maintain the whole household'.[85] Similarly, an IWWU executive statement on the draft constitution referred to the 'vague and chivalrous sentiments of 41.2' and suggested that 'mothers would prefer concrete proposals which would release them from the pressure of economic necessity to work outside the home'.[86] Bennett further conceded that Articles 43 and 45 indicated the right and natural road towards protection of the family and the mother, but felt it preferable to emphasize the father's needs 'as the natural guardian of the family'.[87]

Bennett, with other members of the IWWU executive, formed one of the many deputations to de Valera seeking amendments. The women's groups which joined together to campaign against these clauses in the constitution recognized the potential for discrimination against women in other areas. The recently won franchise, for instance, could be endangered under Article 16 with the removal by de Valera of the words 'without distinction of sex' present in the 1922 constitution. De Valera assured women's groups that he had removed these words only to avoid insulting women by reminding them of how recently they had won this right.[88] Following protests, this clause was re-inserted. Following an IWWU deputation to de Valera in May 1937, Bennett wrote to him noting his commitment to amend Article 45.4 in line with the union's suggestions, but reiterated her dissatisfaction with Article 40.1 which, she stated, 'carried interpretations offensive to a large section of the community and [is] fundamentally different from your own intention'.[89]

De Valera subsequently conceded amendments to Articles 16 and 45 (change to the latter eliminating what the IWWU referred to as 'the obnoxious phrase "inadequate strength of women"', and substitution of the word 'citizen' in place of 'women and children').[90] At this point the IWWU ceased its involvement in the women's campaign against the constitution. The other groups involved, the Women Graduates and the Joint Committee of Women's Societies, were disappointed, recognizing the weakening effect of such action. Rosamund Jacob noted that a meeting of the Joint Committee on 28 May discovered that Bennett, on behalf of women workers, was withdrawing from the campaign 'because she had had private talk with DeV [de Valera] and he was going to alter certain wording, but not, apparently, anything vital'. She noted that the Joint Committee decided to go ahead with its planned public meeting in spite of this.[91] Why did the IWWU abandon the women's cause at this stage? In a letter to *Labour News* Bennett outlined the reasons. Explaining that the IWWU still stood shoulder to shoulder with women's groups fighting for full equal rights for women in Ireland, she pointed out that there was a difference of opinion about the best methods of carrying on that fight.

> My Committee consider that the Amendments to Articles 2, 16 and 45 have removed the really serious menace to the position of women, and that our task now is to direct public opinion in such a way as to prevent any possible attempts to draw from any Section of this Constitution an incitement to sex discrimination.[92]

Bennett stated that the IWWU considered Article 41.2 futile as a mere statement. However, she noted that it could be useful in claiming state support for higher wages, better housing, widows' pensions sufficient to allow widows to live at home with their children, and 'perhaps some form of family allowance payable to the mother'.[93] According to Bennett a woman's trade union owed its first loyalty to the trade union movement as a whole. It was now the task of the IWWU to make male trade unionists realize that it was in the interests of the whole labour movement to establish the principle of equal pay and equal opportunities for women and men.

> We believe that we are advancing steadily towards that desirable position, and we are of [the] opinion that we can best protect ourselves against any dangers inherent in the Constitution by enlisting as our allies in the women's cause those who are already our allies in the great cause of Labour.[94]

Minutes of the IWWU political group noted censure from the Women Graduates Association for their opting out of opposition to those clauses that had not been amended. While agreeing that the social-function clause was very undesirable, the members of the group noted, however, that in view of amendments obtained to Clause 45 following their meeting with de Valera, 'we thought it wise to hold our hand. The matter is to be allowed drop.'[95] Two main considerations prompted this decision. The first was the belief by Bennett and the IWWU executive that their primary responsibility lay with the workers. Their annual report for 1937 stated they were not prepared to engage in a campaign of opposition on the grounds of sex discrimination, pointing out that there were other articles in the constitution which posed more serious threats to the interests of both male and female workers. Ironically, the main thrust of the remaining women's groups campaigning against the constitution was the need to safeguard women's right to work and equal pay. The other main consideration was the status of women within the wider trade union movement. Memories of male trade unionist and Labour Party attitudes during the 1936 controversy were still alive in the minds of the IWWU executive. An alliance with what was disparagingly dismissed as an elite of intellectual middle-class women campaigning for sex equality would not have helped IWWU's efforts to improve women's status within Labour. Crucial too was the acceptance by Bennett and her executive of contemporary Church and state attitudes regarding the role of women in the home.

Public reaction during this controversy reflected popular attitudes to women at work which accepted that after marriage women's place was in the home. Legislation during the 1930s consistently restricted the employment of married women in the public service. Parallel with this was the acceptance of three different pay rates for the same work, for married men, single men and single women, the latter being the lowest. It was also accepted that women should not be promoted beyond basic grades. In 1932, arguing against the Civil Service marriage ban, Mary Kettle commented that 'from their entry until they reach the age of 45 or 50 women are looked upon as if they were loitering with intent to commit a felony, the felony being marriage'.[96] Of particular significance was the fact that many women trade unionists accepted restrictions on the employment of married women, and the often ambivalent attitude of Bennett and the IWWU executive reinforced such acceptance.

Throughout her life Louie Bennett argued trenchantly for equal rights for women in political, social, educational and professional spheres.

However, her 1919 stance that under the then existing industrial system women workers could not fight for equality without regard for wives and mothers, alongside her assurance that women would not invade men's industrial preserves, displayed a personal attitude consistent with conservative popular opinion. In her presidential address to the ITUC in 1932, Bennett had outlined concerns about the growing numbers of women and girls employed in industry as a result of increased mechanization. Pointing out that always these were employed at a lower wage than men, she commented that this practice had debased the workers' standard of life, reduced purchasing power, thereby intensifying unemployment. Again, her argument was double-edged:

> Naturally I have no desire to put a spoke in the wheel of women's employment. But this modern tendency to draw women into industry in increasing numbers is of no real advantage to them. It has not raised their status as workers nor their wage standard. It is a menace to family life, and in so far as it has blocked the employment of men it has intensified poverty amongst the working class.[97]

Mary Daly has pointed to the mental confusion which persisted in this regard within the IWWU into the 1950s.[98] Its 1953 Congress, for example, supported an equal pay proposal but sought to debar from its benefits both young married woman and single women. Jim Larkin reacted to this contradictory action by commenting that before any success could be achieved, 'women would have to propagate the idea of the principle among their own sex and get acceptance for it'.[99] Similarly, Larkin's motion to Dáil Éireann promoting equal pay did not receive the vote of any woman TD, even though, as he pointed out, they received equal pay with their male colleagues. Undoubtedly the attitude of Louie Bennett and the IWWU regarding full economic equality was short-sighted and in the long term damaging to the position of women in Irish society.

The campaign against the trade union Bill of 1941 was another issue which absorbed Bennett's time and energy. This Bill sought to whittle away smaller unions and to eliminate trade union multiplicity. Under its provisions, trade unions would have to register, obtain a government licence to negotiate, and lodge a deposit with the High Court. Concurrent with this Bill the government passed a wages-standstill order, putting a stay on wages from 7 May 1941. Viewing the Bill as 'an attack on the right of workers to form and join unions of their choice without undue interference from the State', the Dublin Trades Council formed a

Council of Action to campaign against both initiatives.[100] This council included members of affiliated unions and the Labour Party. Addressing the annual general meeting of the IWWU, Bennett told members that the Bill was 'the thin edge of fascism, and a very serious threat to the independence of workers'. She joined other trade unionists in an open-air protest meeting at College Green against the Bill in June 1941. At this she stated that:

> This trade union bill has no moral foundations. It is based on the capitalistic ideal that wealth is power. We have won our position today through spiritual force and great sacrifice, and we refuse this Bill because it is fundamentally immoral.[101]

Her executive argued that a union such as theirs, with low-paid workers resulting in low contribution rates, was particularly vulnerable regarding the lodgement of funds with the high court. They also issued a leaflet claiming the blessing of Pope Leo XIII, whose encyclical *Rerum Novarum* had warned workers against state interference. The IWWU also rejected the wages-standstill order, pointing to the hardship imposed on large sections of poorly paid workers at a time of soaring prices. Despite strong opposition from the Council of Action and the IWWU, the new Bill was passed. Following the Trade Union Congress in July 1941, Bennett launched a scathing attack on William O'Brien. Commenting that at no time since 1916 had a Congress met under such menacing circumstances, she claimed that the appropriate leadership had not been provided. In particular she criticized the lack of attention to the problems of unemployment, food prices and fuel shortages, which 'for us women hit right home to our closest interests'. Bennett noted women delegates' shocked bewilderment at O'Brien's hustling through the sections of the report dealing with such issues, 'without giving the delegates an instant's pause even to turn the pages of the report'. On his similar treatment of resolutions regarding these issues, she reported, 'we walked out of the Congress as a protest against this contemptuous treatment of matters acutely affecting trade union interests'.[102]

In 1942 the IWWU applied for and was granted a negotiating licence. While the Council of Action had failed in its key objectives, its work paved the way for co-operation between unions and Labour, and undoubtedly greatly assisted Labour victories in the 1942 local and 1943 general elections. Furthermore, its interest in a broad spectrum of social problems led to a coalition of forces that would function most effectively again in 1946. Part three of the 1941 Act had proposed the establishment of a tribunal empowered to grant one or more unions sole rights to negotiate for certain categories of workers. This had obvious implications for a union such as the IWWU. Following an appeal to the supreme court in 1945, the IWWU scored a significant victory when that court overturned a decision to award the Irish Bookbinders and Allied Trades Union sole organizing rights for all bookbinders on the basis that this contravened the constitutional right to free association. The IWWU, and other smaller unions, benefited from this decision in their fight against absorption by larger unions.[103]

Throughout her involvement with the IWWU, Bennett, together with her executive colleagues, consistently sought improved pay and conditions for a variety of women workers. Where possible such improvements were obtained by negotiation, Bennett's preferred method. Often she knew employers personally, and did not hesitate to use this advantage for the benefit of the union. Fox recounts an incident when she was in a picket line outside a factory striking for higher pay. It happened that Bennett knew the employer socially. When he arrived on the scene, and saw Bennett walking up and down in the rain, he immediately held his umbrella over her. She chided him that it was more important that his staff get a decent wage than she be protected from the rain. Both continued to walk up and down discussing the union demands until agreement was made – all the time under his umbrella. Another employer who dealt with her across the negotiating table was her niece Christabel's husband, Robert (Bobby) Childers. Childers recalled that Bennett treated him exactly as she would any other employer, noting that employers trusted Bennett, aware that when she made a bargain she kept it.[104] But when necessary, strikes there were, and none more noteworthy than the laundry workers' strike during the 1940s.

In 1945 laundry-worker members of the IWWU voted for strike action to obtain a fortnight's paid holiday. Laundresses had sought increased holidays, reduction in overtime, and regular working hours since 1934. Such claims had been shelved during the war years, employers refusing to negotiate. An exception to this was the Court Laundry which, in 1944, unofficially agreed to a second week's paid holiday. As a result the Court was the only laundry to function during the strike. Now the claim for two weeks' holiday became a political issue. Working conditions in laundries were particularly bad. Eleanor Butler (later Lady Wicklow) recounted Louie Bennett taking her on a tour of Dublin laundries:

> She made me wade into the steamy laundries, with floors flooded. The women wore overalls and nothing underneath because they couldn't stand the heat and the steam. They sometimes wore wellingtons if they were lucky, if not battered old shoes. Their conditions were appalling, so much that a very high proportion of these women got TB and suffered from rheumatism.[105]

The IWWU placed much emphasis on the health risks involved in laundry work, arguing that shorter hours and extra holidays were necessary to minimize such risks. In rejecting IWWU demands, the Federated Union of Employers (FUE) intimated that no increased holidays would be granted until the government declared a statutory fortnight's paid holiday. The Minister for Industry and Commerce informed the Dáil of his opposition to any such concession. Despite discussions between the ITUC and the FUE, no resolution was reached. On 21 July 1945, 1,500 women commenced strike action that would last fourteen weeks. Bennett laid the blame for the strike directly on the shoulders of the employers. Writing to the press she made it quite clear that the FUE, and not the IWWU, was responsible for the deadlock.[106] Before the advent of the home washing machine, laundry customers were both domestic and commercial. Despite the great inconvenience caused, it soon became clear that the striking women had public opinion on their side. No opportunity for publicity was missed. Writing to the *Irish Times*, four of the striking women complained of the lack of coverage of the dispute, commenting that the '*Irish Times* is too grand for dirty linen'. This led to the well-known columnist Patrick Campbell ('Quidnunc') visiting the IWWU and detailing their demands in his column. His column returned to the issue a number of times reporting humourously, but scathingly, on the labour-intensive daily routine of a laundry worker.[107] Despite the fact that at this time the trade union movement was torn by dissent, and had in fact split into rival congresses, support for the strikers came from all sides. A watchful eye was also being kept on poaching of commercial laundry work by institutional laundries, particularly convents. The strikers themselves kept morale going with regular meetings, parades, media coverage – and the sale of a strike song, sung to the air of the wartime song 'Lily Marlene', sold at 1d a sheet. Mai Clifford, a participant in the strike, later recounted that 'efforts to dampen such enthusiasm were pressed by the employers through various media campaigns waged against the general secretary, Louie Bennett'.[108] Ultimately the women were successful in their claim, and, as in the case of official tea-breaks introduced some years earlier, set an example quickly followed by male workers. Labour historians have pointed out that without the action of the laundry workers at this time no agreement regarding increased holidays would have been reached, and that their success benefited many other groups of workers. Clifford noted that the successful outcome of the strike 'gave an enormous boost to the union and heightened the profile of the IWWU as a militant and progressive union'.

Reflecting on the achievements of women workers to a teachers' group in 1947, Bennett recounted the horrific conditions of women workers in 1917, underpaid and exploited, working a fifty-four hour week, sixty in laundries, with no paid holidays. She credited women for the considerable reforms achieved in working conditions over the previous thirty years, pointing out that:

> It was the women who inflamed the campaign which won shorter working hours, the extension of the annual holiday, the break in the five-hour shift. And it is the women workers who are leading the drive for amended factory laws, a higher standard of health services and of hygienic environment. Women's influence has in fact proved a humanising factor in industry.[109]

Then in her late seventies, Bennett continued actively to promote that 'humanising factor' and used every means at her disposal.

5

The later years

Approaching her seventieth birthday in 1940, it might have been expected that Bennett would reduce her involvement in public affairs. On the contrary, the 1940s was a particularly busy decade for her. In addition to her work on the Trade Union Bill of 1941 and the laundry workers' strike of 1945, the Commission on Vocational Organization, established by de Valera's government in 1939, took up much of her time and attention. The formation of this Commission followed debate during the 1930s arising from the publication in 1931 by Pope Pius XI of his encyclical, *Quadragesimo Anno.* Joe Lee has commented that this encyclical engendered the first serious sustained discussion of social principles in the history of Irish Catholicism. In the encyclical, a middle path between the extremes of *laissez-faire* capitalism and totalitarian communism was recommended as a corporatist or vocational way. Under such a system:

> Occupational groups would elect self-governing corporations, which would cooperate closely together to wield effective social and economic power throughout society. Corporatism would thus curb class conflict and counter the growing threat to individual liberty from state bureaucracy.[1]

While de Valera would have agreed with much of the ideological thrust of the encyclical, the implicit restraint on political power arising from such a system caused him reservations. However, as Lee points out, he could not afford to appear indifferent to papal teaching. Following a 1936 minority report of a commission on the second house of the Oireachtas recommending the incorporation of a vocational element into Senate elections, de Valera showed interest in the idea. Women's groups, including the Joint Committee of Women's Societies and the IWWU, were active in seeking increased representation for women in the proposed second chamber. Bennett wrote to de Valera a number of times in this regard. Noting that de Valera favoured a vocational basis of representation for the second chamber, she suggested that a certain proportion of women should be appointed to each of the four panels, and that a minimum of four women be among the president's ten nominees. In addition, she advised that a fifth panel be established to represent public health and social services. Noting the increasing importance of this area to public life, one in which women had devoted special care, she argued that 'adequate representation of this department of life in a Second House would give to women the opportunity to promote the objectives which most strongly appeal to them'.[2] De Valera's subsequent constitution of 1937 retained the vocational aspiration of Article 45 of the 1922 constitution, suggesting the new senate would be based on such a system. The women's demands met with little success. Astrid McLaughlin has pointed out that de Valera had suggested to a women's deputation early in 1937 that 'Any inadequacy in the representation of women in the legislature and in public bodies was attributable to the state of public opinion,' and that, 'It would be difficult to do anything to give women a larger place in public life while public opinion remains as it is.'[3] Rosamund Jacob noted the deputation's impression that de Valera was unwilling to do anything to secure any representation for women, saying they had no public opinion behind them, and made difficulties to everything they suggested. Jacob commented, 'He badly needs to be taught a lesson, if there were only enough women with the guts to do it.'[4]

Following a proposal in the Senate in 1938, de Valera agreed to the establishment of a commission of enquiry into vocational organisation. The Commission on Vocational Organization sat from 1939 to 1943, and Bennett was one of twenty-five appointees. There were significant misgivings within Labour circles about the terms of reference of the commission, many identifying corporatism with fascism. Aware of such misgivings, the IWWU annual report noted that:

> It is possible to find in this proposal a suggestion of the Fascist system of Industrial Corporations. Hence Labour's anxiety. Your Secretary will give careful study to the subject and will be strengthened by the fact that she has behind her the knowledge and experience of such an organisation as the Irish Women Workers' Union.[5]

The report was also critical of the fact that only three women had been appointed to the Commission. In addition to written submissions, some 174 groups gave oral evidence to the commission, including the IWWU and the Joint Committee of Women's Societies. The published report of the commission, totalling 539 pages, includes women generally under two sections: 'Personal services – persons engaged in home duties'; and 'The Irish Women Workers' Union'. Apart from the latter, women *per se* are not listed in its fifteen-page index. 'Personal services' included urban and rural women in the home, domestic servants, and workers in the hotel, boarding house and catering trade.[6]

Michael Browne, Catholic Archbishop of Galway, chaired the commission and was particularly aggressive in his questioning of women's groups, represented by the Joint Committee of Women's Societies and Social Workers, the National Council of Women of Ireland, and the Catholic Women's Federation of Secondary School Unions. While witnesses from these groups argued the necessity for the representation of women as 'homemakers', Browne consistently sought to reveal a hidden agenda on their part. He asked when precisely did one become a homemaker, was it on the birth of children? In reply he was told 'when one has to take charge of a home My Lord'.[7] The women further explained that many unmarried women must be classified as homemakers as would some men. Asked if they sought 'territorial principal of organisation for homemakers', the women responded 'We feel that it would be necessary to group them according to their vocation as homemakers, and also in the circle of their local interest to give them some standing and interest in local affairs'.[8] Responding to a comment by one member of the commission panel, Fr. E.J. Coyne, that they ought not to put forward 'being a woman' as a specialized vocation, the women replied that homemaking was a vocation, and not exclusive to women.[9] Asked what type of work women homemakers would be interested in, the women's deputation gave examples of their current involvement. These included the establishment of baby clinics with classes to teach new mothers how to care for their babies, the issue of clean milk, and provision of nursery schools to care for older children where mothers had to work outside the home. The chairman's response was that this smacked of slum work done by the upper classes. Bennett intervened at one stage to point out that, 'In order that the home and the family can be efficiently organised and managed it is necessary for women to carry out a certain amount of social work; they must go out of their homes in order to do the social work.'[10]

Questioning their commitment to women as 'homemakers', Browne asked if all such groups were not feminist or suffragist in origin, whose real aim was the achievement of equality with men. Lucy Kingston replied that women did indeed seek equality. Browne and other men on the Commission continually referred to 'leisured ladies, philanthropists, & slumming do-gooders'. Challenged over his use of the word 'leisured', Browne replied, 'I used the word in the technical sense only to distinguish it from commercial and industrial occupations. Those people of leisure are people who have not to work for a living. That is the ordinary accepted sense of it?' Mrs Dempsey replied that she did not think that would hold, as many of their members worked for a living in different occupations, professions and trades.[11]

While strongly arguing the case for women's representation as homemakers, no dichotomy was seen in differentiating between those who worked outside the home in paid employment, and those who worked full-time in the home, without pay, and who were by implication leisured. While the chairman asked at one stage what organization represented women just as women, no such question was asked of male groups. When Helena Molony, in reply, listed a number of boards and commissions without female representation, including one regarding summer-time with implications for children, a member of the Commission responded that perhaps children should also be asked to serve on the commission.[12]

Bennett was particularly involved when the issue of women workers was under discussion. Four officers of the IWWU gave evidence before the Commission. Archbishop Browne probed the implications of women at work, suggesting that the rise in factory employment for women contributed to male unemployment, and in fact acted as a deterrent to marriage. The IWWU strongly refuted such suggestions, pointing out that union policy reflected feminist attitudes towards life, and that human needs, physical, moral and mental, were more important than money. Molony stated that the IWWU was desperately concerned with the question of male unemployment 'because we regard women as the greater part of the family and where the men are unemployed the women suffer. We are concerned with women not merely as wage earners but primarily as human beings.'[13] Interestingly, in view of the emphasis placed by commissioners and witnesses alike on the importance of woman as homemaker, reflecting current social mores, Helena Molony informed Browne, 'We all believe that woman's place is in the home provided she has a home.'[14] This echoed sentiments expressed in the IWWU annual report for 1938 which stated, 'We are often told that women's place is in the home. We agree that is her special sphere. But war and social injustice are both enemies of the home. It is in order to defend the home and family that women must now take a larger part in public and politics.' Bennett's comments centred mainly on the issue of women at work, within both the IWWU and other unions. She detailed the number of very small factories, in effect sweated workshops, in which women worked in awful conditions. Responding to the claim that men were being ousted by women in the clothing industry, Bennett pointed out that in fact, 'the women have cooperated with the men in reserving the better paid jobs for men in the tailoring trade'.[15] Referring to the difficulties of organizing women workers, she stated that the greatest difficulty was the degree of intimidation to which women were subjected if they attempted to unionize. During the Workers' Union of Ireland submission, Bennett again raised the issue of separate organization for women. Strongly challenging Jim Larkin Junior on this issue, she asked:

> Is it not a fact that but for the Irish Women Workers' Union, women would not be heard of in industry at all? How many of the unions have women on their committees. We are told that it is because women do not take an interest, but it is extraordinary that we have a committee of 15 women who have meetings regularly and deal with their own business. Why therefore are women not considered capable of organising and doing business in other unions? [16]

The Commission's report was presented to government in 1943 and published in 1944. Only two of the four labour representatives signed it, Bennett and Senator Sean Campbell. Both did so after appending a reservation. In this, both explicitly distanced themselves from any potential fascist implications that might be read into the report. Noting that the report aimed at optimum benefits for the community whilst preserving the freedom and rights of the individual, their reservation stated:

> This care for individual freedom is the crucial point of difference between Fascism and vocational organisation. Under Fascism the individual becomes a cog in the machine. Under vocational organisation as envisaged in this Report, he is endowed with the responsibility of service to a vocation and of sharing in the control of its administration . . . Final control of national welfare remains in the hands of a democratically

> elected Parliament . . . The individual citizen will retain his franchise rights not merely as a worker, but as a citizen with many varied interests.[17]

They made the point that while the report offered safeguards against totalitarian developments, they felt it necessary to emphasize their belief that the one reliable safeguard was the conservation of freely elected parliamentary institutions and of the subordination of the executive government to Parliament. Both also considered that the report did not adequately protect consumers, commenting that:

> We are not satisfied that under the existing social system the common good will take precedence of the special interests of any particular vocation. We grant that the profit motive must continue to operate to a certain extent and in certain directions. But it must be subject to control.[18]

In this regard they included a number of recommendations covering agriculture, industry, transport, finance, social services and the proposed provisional assembly. In addition they strongly disagreed with the report's findings regarding externally controlled unions. This had recommended that all associations of workers be required to be completely national. While accepting that the development of vocational organization would eventually involve trade union reorganization, Bennett and Campbell declared, 'we cannot subscribe to any proposals which would infringe upon the right of the workers to choose their own forms of organisations. We claim that the task of reorganisation belongs to the Trade Union Congress.'[19]

Interestingly, Bennett's reservation made no direct reference to women, except in so far as women would be included in the trade union movement. Another member of the commission, Miss M. McGeehin, did attach an addendum to the report on behalf of those engaged in home duties, calling for adequate representation of women as homemakers within the proposed national vocational assembly. It may be that McGeehin and Bennett had agreed that each would enter a reservation/addendum dealing with separate dimensions of the Commission's recommendations, or it may be that Bennett preferred to comment on areas specifically related to her position as a representative of trade unionism. Bennett would no doubt have been aware that some trade union contemporaries were nervous of her views regarding corporatism, at best seeing these as romantic idealism. Bennett had argued in the labour journal, *The Torch,* in 1939:

> We ought not to turn down the theory of Vocational Organisation only because of its resemblance to the Corporative system . . . I do not want to minimise the dangers to the workers [which] are very real, but I confess that I believe [Vocational Organisation] to be worthy of careful study as a natural evolution of industrial development [offering] a way of approach to the goal of industry controlled by the workers, manual and intellectual.[20]

She went on to emphasize that the crux of the problem was in control, commenting that the 'trade union movement can only accept a corporative organisation which is based on co-operative principles and accepts the trade union as a factor in management'. Bennett warned trade unionists:

> A few years ago we were all in a ferment over the communist scare. That has died down. But we ought to be more perturbed by the fascist scare, for fascist ideology is steadily taking root in this country as in others. It is called by more polite names, but it is the same bug.[21]

Towards the end of her life, Bennett wrote of her experience of this Commission. She noted that they had hoped to establish a new 'ism', an ideology which would put Ireland and every small nation on the road to Utopia:

> I remember walking up Merrion Square with Father Hayes after an exciting morning session and we jubilantly told each other that this Commission had found the talisman to inspire a new world society, and that Vocational Organisation would queer the pitch for Communism, State Socialism, Capitalism.[22]

Lee has noted that the Commission's commitment to corporatism was more visceral than intellectual, and that its report in no way supported fascism:

> Its prime purpose was to guard against the dangers of totalitarianism from the right as well as from the left . . . The organisational structure envisaged by the Commission for the vocational system in Ireland was not based on Italian, or even on Portuguese corporatism. There were some superficial resemblances, but neither the composition of the component parts, nor the authority vested in them, corresponded closely to Mediterranean models . . . The Commission stressed that its ideal was not a corporate state, but a corporate society.[23]

Lee has commented that while the report was utopian in certain respects, it was not a crank document, stating that, 'Behind all the anti-materialist rhetoric lay a passionate commitment to material progress, as long as this reinforced rather than subverted Christian values.' He considers the report 'a remarkable document' despite its many inherent weaknesses, and points to the influence to some degree of its recommendations in the formation over the coming years of bodies such as the National Industrial and Economic Council, the Labour Court, Law Reform Commission, and labour–employer conferences.

During the war years Louie Bennett was involved in a series of developments relating to workers' housing and their rights to organize. Her interest in housing had first been articulated during her suffrage days. Consistently over the years, when the issue of working-class housing was raised, she argued that such housing must be of good quality. Writing to Hanna Sheehy Skeffington in the early 1920s regarding possible involvement of the White Cross committee in a proposed housing scheme in Belfast, Bennett stated:

> So far as I can judge, these houses would be of a very inferior character, and must become mere slums in the near future. I object strongly to perpetuating this kind of house for the working people and I question the rightness of White X [sic] funds being devoted to a scheme which can't prove really economic from any point of view. I am very keen that we women should show ourselves alert in regard to [such] schemes.[24]

In a 1925 article headed 'The Order of To-day – Build!', Bennett advocated slum clearance for both medical and moral reasons. Among a number of factors she cited as indicating a positive public approach to this problem, she listed raised public awareness of overcrowded slums allied to concern for public health, and the fact that, increasingly, working-class women would not accept inferior housing. On the latter point she noted that within the IWWU the question of housing 'is one of intense interest and never fails to arouse prolonged and keen discussion'.[25] A number of initiatives were undertaken by the IWWU in this regard during the 1920s and 30s, but plans for direct union investment in the late 1930s had to be abandoned due to spiralling costs. Jones has cited a series of stinging letters by Bennett to *The Torch* outlining the causes of such price increases and the extent of corruption within the building trade.[26] IWWU executive minutes from 1938 show concern at Dublin Corporation's proposed rent system for new local authority houses, its executive protesting to the Dublin Trades Council that 'a system by which the poor are segregated into special areas, according to the rent they are able to pay savours of class distinction'.[27] Bennett consistently placed a high priority on this matter, recruiting young architects like Eleanor Butler, and forming the Citizens' Housing Council with Father Canavan and Dr Bob Collis.[28] Towards the end of her career she continued to take an uncompromising stand on the necessity of providing adequate housing for the low paid, leading a deputation to Leinster House in this regard. Ultimately, due to her perseverance and support, a development of such houses was built close to her home in Ballybrack.[29]

A number of women's groups came together during the war years seeking a fair rationing system to cope with wartime shortages of essential goods. Bennett and the IWWU supported their demands. The years of 'The Emergency' saw prices soar and goods become prohibitively expensive. No policy of rationing had been introduced, and children and the elderly particularly suffered malnutrition and disease. Emmet O'Connor has pointed out that during these years the cost of living rose by two-thirds while wages rose by one-third. He notes that a combination of unemployment, poverty, and the social inequality of the Emergency regime, swung public opinion to the left.[30] A group of women headed by Hilda Tweedy and Andrée Sheehy Skeffington put together a petition demanding equality in production and distribution of food, fair prices for both consumer and producer, and immediate effective rationing. They also sought a free milk scheme for pregnant and nursing mothers, a rise in unemployment allowances, and the familiar demand from suffrage days for communal kitchens and restaurants. The petition presented to government by this group before the 1941 budget was dubbed 'The Housewives' Petition' by the press. Bennett advised the group's leaders to build on the momentum generated by the petition and start a new women's organization, offering the use of the IWWU hall for its inaugural meeting. So was formed the Irish Housewives' Association in May 1942.[31] Hanna Sheehy Skeffington was unhappy with the word 'Housewife' in the title of the new group, telling her daughter-in-law Andree, 'You are not married to the house, you know'. Bennett appears to have had no problem with the title, perhaps echoing her very traditional attitude toward women and housekeeping. During the First World War, writing of wartime work available to women, Bennett had criticized the government for not utilizing women 'even in departments for which her special training and experience make her peculiarly adapted'. Subsequently, during her 1920 editorship of the

Irish Citizen, she was embroiled in controversy over her inclusion of a 'home hints column'. Due to her abrupt departure as editor, her intended series of articles on 'The mistress and the maid problem' never materialized. Yet it would appear that, for some years to come, this issue was still a matter of debate. The subject arose again in 1943 when Maura Laverty wrote in *The Bell* on 'Maids versus Mistresses'. Referring to recent correspondence in Dublin newspapers on this matter, Laverty told readers that Bennett and the IWWU had again attempted the organization of domestic workers and wardsmaids. This had led to the formation of the Domestic Employers' Association. It was hoped that agreement would be reached between the two groups on a common code governing hours of work, annual leave and a minimum accommodation standard. Laverty pointed out that some years earlier Bennett had presented a training scheme for such workers to the government, but had received no encouragement.[32] The IWWU annual report for 1937/38 noted that a meeting with the Department of Industry and Commerce in this regard had been 'coldly received and the position remains the same'. That report went on to observe that, 'If woman's place is in the home and by the cradle, had she not better learn how to keep the home and mind the baby?'

Three years later Bennett herself put pen to paper on 'The domestic problem'. Advising Irish housewives to consider how they would reorganize their home-keeping in mind of the forthcoming domestic revolution, she commented: 'Such a revolution is already at our doors. Domestic service as known in the middle-class paradise of Victorian days is gone forever.' The revolution she referred to was not the replacement of servants by appliances, but rather a change in relationship, as she noted, 'The "mistress and maid" theory has become an employer–employee problem surrounded by uncomfortable restrictions.' Observing that the move towards organisation and minimum standards of wages, hours and working conditions had not progressed as far in Ireland as in other countries, she felt that drastic reform would happen in the not too distant future. Arguing that, 'the gates of the home will not prove a barrier to the onward march of the social revolution [which] is psychological in origin and inextricably linked with human relationships', she maintained that this revolution sprang primarily from workers' resentment against their subject status and lack of power to control their lives. She further argued that workers or 'employed persons' now sought, consciously or subconsciously, equality of status, the position of co-operator rather than of hired labourer, the objective of service to the community as the primary motive of employment'. Implicitly accepting woman's role as housewife, Bennett maintained that the nature of that role as employer had changed. Both the housewife and the domestic helper would have to view domestic service as a service to the community just as valuable as the Civil Service:

> The woman who sets up a home herself enters upon a form of domestic service and becomes thereby a servant of the community. The domestic help who comes into the home to co-operate in its service must hold an equal professional status with the housewife herself. The fact of the exchange of labour for money cannot affect that status.

Bennett noted that the housewife would be helped in this process of change by the growing tendency to attach to the home and the family a very important and special function in human life. Unsure as to what woman's place in the new mechanised world would be, Bennett concluded that:

> Our line of hope lies in a new approach to the home and the domestic sphere, and if the new generation accept home-keeping as a vocation and a social service I believe they will blaze a trail towards a finer civilisation than we have yet known.[33]

Bennett's article implied that women should adopt a more positive and articulate attitude to their role within the home. Echoing arguments put forward by women's groups to the commission on vocational organization, she saw woman's domestic role as an important community service. Where she differed from points put forward in that forum was in her arguments for an equality of status for domestic workers. She does not appear to have foreseen a situation whereby existing patterns of domestic employment would be reversed by technical developments and female emigration. Nor does she refer to the payment of woman – the employer – the housewife, for her services. In arguing for home-keeping to be viewed as a social service on a par with the Civil Service, she ignored any financial consideration. Even her brief reference to possible payment to women in the home made during the 1937 controversy surrounding the constitution was not included here. Emphasis was placed on the role of home-keeper as a vocation, albeit an enlightened one regarding domestic employees. Interestingly, in 1935 the executive of the IWWU had received a subscription towards its political fund from a Mrs Nicholls, but their report notes that as 'she is not a worker in the earning sense we cannot accept her donation, and will advise her to join the Labour Party'.[34]

During the 1940s, Bennett made a number of attempts to enter politics. She was elected to Dun Laoghaire Borough Council in August 1942, but was unsuccessful in her attempt to be elected as a Labour candidate in the general election of 1944. In 1938 she had been nominated to Congress as a Senate candidate by the IWWU executive and the Textile Operatives' Society of Ireland. This too proved unsuccessful due to a subsequent congress decision to withdraw as a nominating body.[35]

When a split occurred in the Labour Party in 1944, with serious consequences for the trade union movement, Bennett used all her influence to bring about a reconciliation. The initial split centred on the admission of both Jim Larkin Senior and Jim Larkin Junior to the Labour Party in December 1941, and their subsequent election to the Dáil in 1943. Opposition by the ITGWU, fuelled by long-running enmity between Larkin Senior and William O'Brien, led to the ITGWU seceding from the Labour Party to form the National Labour Party in January 1944. Now a member of Labour's administrative council, Bennett contacted Tom Johnson in February that year, appealing to him to intervene in the dispute. Recounting that she had shared the platform with Norton, Connolly and Larkin Junior at the Labour Party election rally in the Mansion House when Larkin Senior was nominated, Bennett explained that she had accepted this action 'as the lesser of two evils'. Both she and Connolly had subsequently used all their influence to prevent Larkin Junior being expelled from the party, acknowledging that they were equally deserving of condemnation. Accepting that compromise would have to be made on both sides, she stated that both Larkins would have to be accepted by the ITGWU leadership into the Labour Party, commenting that the 'communist bogey has nothing to do with it'. Appealing to Johnson to act as appeaser, Bennett noted, 'You saved the trade-union movement in 1916. Can you help the Labour Party now?'[36] Following the establishment of a separate trade union congress in 1945, named the Congress of Irish Unions, Bennett continued to do all in her power to bring about unity. During the period of dual congresses, which lasted until 1959, the IWWU remained within the original ITUC. In 1946 Bennett was again elected vice-president of that Congress, and the following year was elected president for the second time. In the course of her presidential address in 1948 she outlined her concerns for trade unionism within Ireland. Regarding relations between Labour and government, with particular reference to Labour's current participation in the inter-party government coalition, Bennett declared:

> If trade unionists fail now to direct and control the development of their own movement towards a defined objective, then the Government will take the initiative and provide themselves with powers to control and use it for their own purposes. Whatever professions liberal politicians may make regarding freedom and democracy the drift towards totalitarian methods of State control persists.[37]

She also referred to necessary organizational changes needed within Congress, pointing to the emergence of the Federated Union of Employers and the Labour Court as indicative of the need for specialization and expertise. In this regard she proposed increased powers and financial support to the Congress executive. True to character, Bennett also discussed international problems. Her distrust of the Marshall Plan and of American aid to Europe was voiced, as was her concern at tensions between the United States and Russia which resulted in investment needed for economic development being used for military purposes. Her constant theme of internationalism recurs when she urged trade unionists – north and south – to become involved in international affairs, stating, 'Isolationism is an extinct policy.' Not a message to be accepted easily in a country recently marked by closed xenophobic anxiety, economic protectionism and a strong authoritarian disposition.[38] Thanking Bennett for her inspiring address, James Larkin observed that, to those who had worked closely with her on the national executive, it was not surprising that she had presented a mixture of spiritual values as well as current industrial problems. As a veteran of the trade union movement, Bennett, he noted, had set a broad and high level for all delegates to follow.

Emmet O'Connor has described 1946 as 'a watershed in labour history' with the establishment of the Labour Court under the Industrial Relations Act. With wartime pay freezes abolished, pay claims would now be processed through the Labour Court. Bennett, while not completely against the Court, told John de Courcy Ireland that 'my crowd see its dangers and the IWWU did take a lead in looking for safeguards'. Accepting the need for conciliation procedures, but fearing too close a bond with government, she added wryly, 'my generation can never get free of the "ag'in the government" instinct.'[39] The first national pay round awarded that year appeared as good news for workers. Yet there was much concern that pay awards would not keep pace with price increases. A consumer price index of 173 for 1939 had increased to 288 by 1946. To the consumer this meant that goods costing 12 shillings in 1939 cost 20 shillings in 1946.[40] The Dublin Trades Council decided to revive the strategy of the Council of Action and bring together labour and women's groups to campaign for price control. At a conference held in the Mansion House in January 1947, representatives from women's groups were joined by the Labour Party, Clann na Poblachta and Dublin Trades Council. From this was formed the Lower Prices Council (LPC).[41] Offices were established with the help of the Dublin Trade Union Council (DTUC), and intensive investigation was conducted into the price of food, clothing and housing. Writing to Sean Lemass in October that year, Bennett urged that whatever measures government might take regarding prices and rationing should not be restricted to particular groups within society but should apply to all, otherwise such action 'savours of charity'. Similarly, in regard to proposals for utility clothing, she advised him 'it is again essential to avoid the appearance of charity, and also to preserve an element of good style as has been done in England & Northern Ireland. This applies equally to children as to adults, children being extremely sensitive to appearances.'[42] In October that year the LPC organized what became known as 'The Women's Parliament' in the Mansion House. Hilda Tweedy has recounted that:

> The LPC decided that an association of women's organisations could be an effective ally to combat the continuous rise in the cost of living and to work for a betterment of social conditions.[43]

At this meeting, participating women were allocated ministerial portfolios to emphasize their right to commentate on the national housekeeping. Bennett chaired this inaugural meeting, from which was formed the Women's National Council of Action (WNCA) as a subsidiary of the LPC. The WNCA produced six demands relating to the control of rents and food prices and the establishment of producer/consumer markets. As with the laundry workers' strike, public attention was focused on women's demands. Commenting on the idea of a women's parliament in his satirical column in the *Irish Times,* Myles na gCopaleen reported:

> It says in the paper that more than 300,000 women in every county in Ireland will be represented at the Women's Parliament in Dublin – to *demand* – if you don't mind, 'Control of prices and an immediate reduction

> in the cost of essential goods and other commodities.' Hah? I well remember the day, and your poor father would bear me out in this, when into the newspapers the word 'women' never got!! In those days respectability was the rage of course.[44]

Whatever about respectability, the WNCA kept up the pressure to achieve its aims, and in 1949 one of these aims was attained with the establishment by Dublin Corporation of a producer/consumer market in Francis Street. This and the establishment in 1951 of a Prices Advisory Board were two significant achievements of the WNCA. In line with these ideas, consumer co-operatives were established in Inchicore and Ballyfermot. Bennett, long an advocate of the co-operative movement, supported this development. In her tutelage of the young Eleanor Butler, for instance, she had introduced her to the work of Horace Plunkett and of Paddy 'the Cope' Gallagher in Donegal. The IWWU also invested in the new Dublin ventures. The co-operative ran from 1946 to 1952, eventually foundering amidst accusations of communist tendencies. At the height of this controversy – when no other meeting place could be found – Bennett allowed the co-op committee the use of the IWWU hall.[45]

There were other areas of public life that absorbed Bennett's time during the 1940s, among them the building of sanatoria to cope with the enormous public health problem of TB, the provision of worker education, and the establishment of closer links with people in Northern Ireland. Eleanor Butler had been persuaded by Bennett to join the Labour Party, and in the early 1940s was elected to Dublin Corporation. Butler has recounted that Bennett's method was to work behind the scenes – in this way she claimed Bennett exerted enormous influence on the trade union and labour movement. An architect by profession, Butler was appointed to the Housing and Town Planning Committees. She was later appointed to the Board of Newcastle Hospital, having been advised by Bennett to aim for this. Thus Butler learned first-hand about the organization and funding of sanatoria. According to Butler, Bennett planned that the IWWU should build its own sanatorium, and by 1947 she had managed to raise promises of £100,000 in sponsorship from employers and trade unions. Bennett intended approaching the government to match these pledges, and planned a public meeting in the Bakers Hall with the support of John Swift. Shortly before this public meeting, Bennett visited Newcastle with Butler, and was shown around the sanatorium by Dr Noel Browne, Assistant Medical Superintendent. Bennett was so impressed with

Browne that she asked him to be principal speaker at her planned meeting. Browne agreed. Other speakers at the meeting in November 1947 included Sean McBride and Noel Hartnett. Within months, following a general election, Browne was elected to the Dáil and appointed Minister for Health. As such he quickly transformed the face of public medical care for TB sufferers. Butler, and others, have acknowledged the support given to Browne by Bennett, both on the TB issue and during the later 'Mother and Child' controversy. In 1951 Bennett represented the IWWU on deputations to Browne regarding the latter scheme, and privately was much in contact with him during this period. Officially, however, the IWWU let it be known that it was unhappy that no woman doctor had been appointed to the Medical Committee involved with the Mother and Child Scheme.[46]

Butler stood as a Labour candidate in the general election of 1948, again at Bennett's insistence. She was unfortunate that running against her in Dublin South-East were Sean McIntee (Fianna Fáil), John Costelloe (Fine Gael) and Dr Noel Browne (Clann na Poblachta), all three of whom were elected. Butler was subsequently appointed to the Senate as one of the Taoiseach's nominees. She represented the Labour Party there until 1952.

Regarding worker education, Bennett had consistently advocated improved educational facilities for women. While serving on an education committee of the ITUC national executive in 1925 she and Marie Mortished, had moved that girls be included in proposed day training classes for apprentices. In 1927 Bennett and Helen Chenevix gave evidence on behalf of the IWWU at the Saorstat Éireann technical education commission. Among their recommendations were the raising of school leaving age from fourteen to sixteen years, technical education of a domestic character for all girls, training for domestic assistants and agricultural colleges for boys and girls to teach improved farming methods.[47] Following the 1925 ITUC recommendation that a Workers' Educational Institute be formed, evening classes were started, enthusiastically supported by Bennett. The IWWU provided lecture rooms and their hall to the committee. While this initiative lasted only a couple of years, the IWWU executive continued its commitment to the idea, including educational projects in its budget, and provision of a library and classes for members. In 1948, following a proposal by Bennett to the ITUC National Executive, the People's College was founded, with Bennett as one of the key members of its organizing committee. Despite subsequent controversy regarding the ideological bias of the College's constitution, and the vexed issue of non-sectarian education, resulting in a rival workers' college being established by the Jesuits in Ranelagh, the People's College grew in strength with a distinguished team of lecturers and administrators, and the continued support of the IWWU.[48]

From her suffrage days Bennett had always maintained close links with women in Ulster. She had a number of close friends in the province, including Ethel MacNaughton, Mary MacNeill and Fanny Heron. Bennett was a frequent visitor to Ethel MacNaughton who worked to improve the conditions of mill-workers in the province. She brought Eleanor Butler on one such visit, pointing out to her that, 'While these [mill] girls make the most beautiful linen in the world, they have to eat their own meals off newspapers.'[49] Bennett's contact with the northern province was extended during her years with the IWWU and the ITUC. A further link was provided with her involvement in the Irish Association for Cultural, Economic and Social Relations. Branches of this non-party association were formed in Belfast and Dublin during 1938, aiming to promote co-operation and goodwill between Irish people north and south. The outbreak of war in 1939 placed huge strain on the new association, exacerbated by the very different policies to the war adopted by the Belfast and Dublin governments. The association was revived after the war, with Bennett very actively involved in the Dublin branch.[50] Bennett continued to place much emphasis on maintaining and promoting dialogue between all peoples, north and south. The year before her death she wrote to John de Courcy Ireland urging that the Labour Party adopt a gradual approach to the re-unification of Ireland under a four-provinces federal government. As a first step she suggested the establishment of a joint consultative council composed of representatives from all political parties within both parts of Ireland.

Right up to the end of her life Bennett remained keenly involved and interested in all aspects of Irish life and current affairs generally. Letters from her last years show a lively enquiring mind, a person concerned with the individual, encouraging in difficult times, and supportive of independent thought and action. It is clear from her letters – and interviews with family and friends – that she had a keen interest in young people and their views. Young people enjoyed her company, finding her not just a sympathetic listener, but a stimulating and supportive friend. Her nieces and nephews all had warm memories of time spent with her. One niece remembered holidays spent with Bennett in the 1930s when, 'We would sit in front of the fire during the Christmas holidays, eating

Jaffa oranges, hands in front of the fire settling the world.'[51] She was still an avid reader, particularly of books on politics, philosophy and the women's labour movement. Her brother, Lionel, lived with her into the 1940s and was supported by her. He was crippled with arthritis, and, interestingly, relatives recount how Bennett always deferred to his opinions. All remember Bennett's temper, regularly hearing her argue hotly on the telephone. A niece of Helen Chenevix, Helen Allott, noted that her aunt found Bennett's bad humours hard to take, and Allott herself commented that, 'you really ran if you knew she was in bad humour.' Bennett would work herself to the bone and then collapse into bed, unable to understand why things were not done the way she wanted. She had a lot of illness – heart trouble and diabetes – and from time to time under medical advice had to work from her bed. On these occasions, Allott recounts that Bennett, always fussy about her appearance, would be found sitting up in bed with her hair done, in a pretty bed-jacket and nightdress, surrounded by papers and work.[52] She admired those who did a fair day's work, disliking constant moaning.

Her comments to a friend in England set this outlook in a broader context. Describing why she found records of the Brontë family so depressing, Louie commented, 'They are so involved in gloom, and always suffering from headaches or overwork or drab surroundings, no wonder the one brother took to drink!'[53] She disliked deceit, and strongly disapproved of marital infidelity. Her Sunday 'at homes' saw friends and relatives gather at her house in Killiney. Samuel Beckett, whose family home was nearby, was among the regular attenders. She retained her interest in music. Writing to John de Courcy Ireland in 1946, Bennett referred to hearing the Hallé Orchestra, and told him delightedly 'Do you know that Henry Holst is spending August in my house and his Philharmonic Quartet rehearsed in my garrett room last Sunday.' She took a keen interest in the theatre, particularly in the careers of her niece Mary Manning at the Gate in Dublin, and of Mary O'Malley at Belfast's Lyric Theatre. She also encouraged O'Malley's political career, while pointing out to her 'the frightful boredom of a corporation job'.[54] Constantly, she encouraged her correspondents to positive action. Writing to one friend, Seamus Scully, unhappily forced to work in England, Bennett advised 'Don't repine for the loss of Ireland and of your Dublin interests, [but] cultivate an interest in England and the problems of life there and see what you can learn from them.' Scully was a friend of Sean O'Casey, and in this letter Bennett commented of the latter, 'Is'nt [sic] he very foolish to worry so much about his critics!'[55]

On a lighter note, when her friend, author Patricia Lynch, was planning a trip to the races, Bennett advised:

> Be sure you back half a dozen winners on Monday. Don't accept any tips. Run down the list of horses & spot your own favourite – wish I was going with you! I always associate Fairyhouse with rows of outside cars speeding frantically towards it, & the people swaying about on the cars looking as frantic as the horses – how dull to go in a shining motor as you will do![56]

Bennett was quite despondent about the Labour Party during these years, considering the trade union movement much more progressive. Her disenchantment continued into the 1950s. In 1952 she described the Party conference, 'a wash-out, important matters were shelved and we were cornered by the opportunistic politician's cliques'.[57] But, she noted triumphantly, 'We did at least get a spoke in the wheel of another inter-party government.' This quip refers to her earlier strong stance regarding coalition. When a coalition was proposed between Fianna Fáil and Labour in 1927, Bennett was the sole dissenter within the Labour national executive, declaring that, 'Coalition meant a compromise on fundamental principles.'[58] When she learned of the proposal to establish an Irish Management Institute late in 1952, Bennett immediately wrote to Dublin Trades Union Council pointing out that the trade unions had not been invited to participate, even though one of the functions of the proposed institute was to secure satisfactory labour relations.[59] In 1953 she issued a strong directive to union members to participate in a forthcoming protest regarding unorganized Civil Servants and the non-implementation of Civil Service pay awards: 'Don't stand on the sidewalk looking on. March proudly in a demonstration for justice and human rights.'[60]

The Irish Association features frequently in Bennett's letters to Mary O'Malley. Here too she was somewhat impatient of progress, commenting that the organization must move on to bolder objectives than cultural exchanges and mutual compliments. In 1955 she told O'Malley, 'I personally am a wilted reed you know, but I want to see you of the young generation going ahead and confounding all the old fogies so afraid of the new World.'[61] She may have felt a wilted reed, but it is clear that intellectually and psychogically she was still very sharp. Two weeks after her letter to O'Malley, she wrote the Irish Association 'a thundering letter suggesting activities that will terrify them, [that] the time is past for polite meetings, something more stirring is wanted to block

Sinn Féin'. Despairing of politicians apparently unable to supply an alternative policy to Sinn Féin and the IRA, she urged other groups to keep on talking as 'there is a younger generation ready to seize on an ideal with an element of inspiration and hope.'[62] Writing to John de Courcy Ireland in 1953 on the partition debate in the Dáil, she criticized a Labour deputy's apparent challenge to the Protestant community, indicating her intention to prepare a Protestant group to speak out should victimization of Catholics occur in the North following IRA aggression.[63]

By 1955, at the age of 85, Bennett had at last retired from the IWWU, noting 'I live the life of a real lady now. I do nothing & don't want to do anything. To an onlooker without responsibility, life can be tremendously interesting and even exciting.' Her international perspective was still a strong feature, her correspondence indicating her sadness that:

> We remain so isolated from the outside world & so apparently indifferent to the great events likely to revolutionise our system of civilisation. I think the North as well as the South are mentally island bound – they care only for their own interests. Is it that those who have a wider vision become missionaries or emigrants?[64]

In 1955, Bennett was hospitalized for some time. Back home again she told her friend Seamus Scully that she would not mind so much being an awful crock, if only the sun would shine, advising him 'console yourself, you are living through the hardest stage of your life. Old age is not so bad.'[65] Still she kept herself informed, constantly urging others to be active. Much of her attention was absorbed by the development of nuclear power, and she strongly supported opposition to the hydrogen bomb. She wrote to Seamus Scully of her support for Ackland's campaign in this regard, adding characteristically, 'I feel we all ought to be *up and doing* [sic] in the campaign against it'. She urged Scully to contact the Peace Pledge Union and support Ackland's advice that energies be focused on building up a new world in which minds will be set on feeding the hungry peoples and helping the ignorant and feeble to learn to develop their talents and their land. As late as 1954 she informed Mary O'Malley of her plan to organize around her some young people to debate the part Ireland might play in the struggle of the colonies against imperialism, commenting, 'We won't get away from the Atom Bomb threat until the Colonial peoples get fair play.' Constantly she urged her correspondents to get involved in social issues and not sit idly by.[66] One of her last efforts in this regard was her invitation to some thirty people to her house to rally support for the only woman candidate in Dun Laoghaire local authority elections in 1955. She was most disappointed when only ten people turned up.[67]

Bennett's emphasis on spiritual values had been articulated many times over the years. In her presidential address to the ICTU in 1948 she had declared that the trade union, now an integral part of the social fabric, was in origin inspired by spiritual values. Now, at a crossroads in its history, she believed it had a vital part to play in the evolution of a civilization based on such values. In an article published ten years earlier she had criticized the dominating motive of industry as evil from every point of view, declaring that, 'The motive of all work, whether it be of the manager, the expert, the machine minder, the apprentice, needs the element of religion in the sense of service to life.'[68] Her idealistic view that the motive of the artist creating beauty should be the same as that of the street cleaner, mechanic, weaver or politician persevered over the years. Sean O'Faolain, a good friend, teased her and Hubert Butler, noting that both believed in universal love and hated nobody.[69] Writing in *The Bell* in 1951 on the issue of government acceptance of American aid, with possible implications for Ireland, Bennett cited Muintir na Tire, the Young Farmers' and the Irish Countrywomen's associations, and the growing co-operative ideals as positive native phenomena. She believed that the new spirit moving the younger generation, allied to thinkers like O'Faolain would ensure national integrity, and that the Irish 'left free to follow their own way of life' could make a valuable contribution to civilization.[70]

Although Bennett is described by her relatives as not at all religious, the themes of spirituality and religion recur constantly throughout her correspondence. Writing of her interest in studying the individual's need for a foundation to life, she commented that, 'With the loss of church influence and the terrific developments of science, many of us seem to be left rudderless in a stormy world.' In 1950 she wrote to her niece, 'I bore my colleagues by constantly asserting that the restlessness and discontent of the workers arises from a sub-conscious craving for their rights as human persons.'[71] Discussing the surrealist Paul Nash, Louie observed:

> This generation is living through [a] period of destruction, but faith in a new integration for the spirit of man persists. In the heart of the scientist the gleam raises a question – whither life? Why life values? In the heart of the poet, the artist, the quest for interpretation of life, for hidden meanings and treasures. In the heart of the common man . . . the gleam points still to the Holy Grail, the Kingdom of God.[72]

She confided to her niece:

> Every decade of one's life brings the need for some re-adjustment, but especially the middle decades, both for men and women, married and unmarried. We shed then many of youth's hopes and desires and demands, and we face the necessity to make the best of whatever position we may have attained. It's a difficult and often an agonising experience, and very often involves adjustment of our relations with other people. But once having cleared the hurdle, we start with a new (not re-newed) but new input.[73]

Bennett recounted Emily Balch's advice that the best years of one's life are the sixties – all passion spent, futile regrets abandoned, futile hopes forgotten – when one can devote oneself with serenity to one's special task. Bennett had now come to agree with this observation, but commented that the 'serenity' was a bit of a poser. She wrote to her niece of Einstein's theory of a cosmic religion based on order and natural law – all life being inspired by a force which is God, with human religions all being expressions of this Godhead. She identified the Holy Trinity as a 'wonderful symbol of this cosmic religion'. Just months before her death she told her niece, 'As you know I am very unorthodox religiously, and it occurred to me that I ought to think out my position clearly and hand on my reflections to you.' She believed that we lead a double life, on the one hand the material, physical life giving scope of action and energy, on the other an inner life, seeking the unseen – the difficulty being in balancing the two to create harmony. In this regard she recounted reading Simone Weil and Schwitzer. In the course of this letter, Louie Bennett wrote what might have been her epitaph:

> Standing as I do at the end of my life, I have a strange conviction of the *value* [sic] of life. I think of it as a tremendous adventure, carrying a challenge to us. I am glad to have lived, to be a part of life, however insignificant. I have known the dark days of the soul. I look back on failures, & disappointments & contemptible sins of omission & commission, and still I am glad to have lived, and I look ahead to a great future for man. It seems absurd to write this, but I have a conviction about it which rises up against every doubt & is in a sense stronger than myself. I don't want to live in the new world that's coming for the younger generation, but I like to think of it and to hope for a further revelation of God, & that all the present restlessness & seeking for a 'spar' to hold on to will lead to a deeper understanding of the mystery & greatness of life.

Her closing comment to her niece reads, 'I think love outlasts death.'[74]

Conclusion

If the first forty years of Louie Bennett's life remain elusive and something of a mystery, her remaining forty-six years were spent very much in the public domain. Her involvement in the women's suffrage movement, her subsequent high profile within the pacifist movement and above all her trade union career, indicate a woman driven by a mission. What was the spark that fuelled this development on the part of one whose background and early life showed no indication of what was to come? Why at the age of forty-one did she turn her life about so dramatically and enter the public arena? Speaking with the benefit of hindsight, we know that in fact her move into the suffrage movement was the first step in what was to be a varied public career. At the time, no one, least of all Bennett herself, knew what lay ahead. From discussions with her nieces, it is clear that Bennett and her sisters were all keenly interested in the women's movement, one niece describing the Bennett sisters as 'all women's libbers at the time'.[1] Fox noted in his biography that when the issue of women's suffrage was raised in the Bennett household, the brothers were inclined to jeer, 'but the girls, influenced by Louie, ranged themselves on the side of feminist pioneers'.[2] Her keen interest in literature, in particular her reading of authors such as Schreiner and Ibsen, would have informed her growing awareness of the women's issue. Developments within the suffrage movement in Great Britain from the turn of the century, particularly its radicalization under the influence of the Pankhursts, inspired many Irishwomen to become involved. As discussed in Chapter 2, this upsurge of interest manifested itself in different ways through different women's groups, and obviously

Bennett was very much aware of what was happening on the ground. As noted above, she was on the subscription list of the IWSLGA for two years. Yet, rather than take a leading role with any of the existing suffrage societies, she went out and helped to form a new one, ultimately creating her own in the IWRL. Many people who knew Bennett have referred to her leadership skills. It would appear that those qualities were present from the beginning. In addition, a stubborn streak and firm sense of purpose were evident again and again during her subsequent career. She would not be deflected from what she saw as the correct course of action for herself. As another of her nieces remarked, 'Whatever she wanted, she got'.[3]

While the Bennetts appear to have had a comfortable lifestyle, it would seem that there were financial problems from time to time. Perhaps her father's business fluctuated, and a family of nine children plus parents and various maiden aunts, not to mention servants, could cause financial pressure. Bennett was aware of such problems. Fox has noted that in addition to her in-depth reading of well-known authors, she immersed herself in many literary periodicals. One such periodical was *Black and White,* through which she discovered the reviewer Barry Pain. Pain, as noted earlier, became Bennett's writing tutor. While the two novels she subsequently published were not successful in literary terms, their publication displayed Bennett's determination at a time when Pain warned her about the problems facing women authors. The fact that both novels were love stories has raised questions about their inspiration. Family members have referred to one or two possible romantic involvements in Bennett's life. One such suggestion – bearing all the hallmarks of a nineteenth-century romantic novel itself – was that, while keeping house for her brother Lionel in Ballynahinch, County Down, Bennett met and fell in love with a northern newspaper editor. The man's wife was hospitalized due to alcoholism, and he could not divorce her. Bennett's nieces also referred to a possible American love interest. Her sister, Violet, had married an American Navy Captain, and after Violet's early death, Bennett and he kept in touch. Bennett is reputed to have been quite smitten by him. Without firmer evidence it is impossible to prove or disprove either of these supposed dalliances.

In summary, what emerges from the scant material available regarding Bennett's life before forty is a picture of a well-read, articulate woman seeking a means of self-expression. She had not married, had no professional or career training, nor indeed seemed to need such for financial reasons at this time. Her entry into public life in 1911 can be seen as a response to what she viewed as the needs of the suffrage movement. This involvement would soon reveal her organizational skills, allied to her deep commitment to the cause of women.

Once involved in the suffrage movement, Bennett seemed to emerge, butterfly-like into an acknowledged leader of women in various spheres. It is not known for how long or how well she knew other women prominent in the suffrage cause before 1911, but clearly she soon became one of that unique group. Writing contemporaneously in *The Feminist Movement* Ethel Snowden, a British suffragist who worked closely with Irish groups, pointed out that feminism and woman's suffrage were not the same thing, although they were the offspring of the same idea:

> Feminism seeks to remove all barriers which oppose the perfect freedom of women as human beings, conventional, social, political and economic. Women's suffrage would break down one of these barriers only – the political barrier. The difference between women's suffrage and feminism is one of degree rather than kind, but there are differences of degree that constitute almost a difference in kind.[4]

Bennett would undoubtedly have considered herself a feminist within the Snowden's definition. In 1919 she noted that 'the suffrage campaign [had been] little more than a preliminary skirmish in a big progressive movement [towards] women's struggle for her place in the world'.[5] In an examination of the evolution of feminism in Western societies, Karen Offen has written of two distinct schools, the relational and the individualist. The former accepted a gender-based but egalitarian vision of society, based on a non-hierarchical, male–female couple as the base unit, while the latter concentrated more on personal independence in all aspects of life, downplaying or dismissing as insignificant all socially defined roles.[6] Bennett would appear to fall within the former category. Attainment of the vote she believed would enable women to influence and help develop a more humane society. During her involvement in the pacifist movement from 1915, Bennett articulated views similar to those of Jane Addams and Emmeline Pethick-Lawrence, that women as custodians of life should join together to ensure that the militarist system be replaced by a pacifist system of conciliation. Women would be able to initiate such change only through the power of the vote, allied to international co-operation and organization by women's groups worldwide. Post-suffrage, Bennett's efforts to improve the status, pay and conditions of women workers was grounded in acceptance of the family unit, with particular emphasis on the potential power of the 'mother element' in reforming society. In this regard, a distinct contrast can be made between Bennett and Hanna Sheehy Skeffington. While both sought the active involvement of women in public life, Sheehy Skeffington consistently opposed the implicit societal definition of women's familial role. Bennett's subsequent career indicates her acceptance of that role, while simultaneously attempting to ameliorate living and working conditions.

Within four years of her initial involvement, Bennett's contribution to the women's movement was dramatically extended by her strong anti-militarist stance both internationally, and more problematically, in a domestic context. In his study of European feminism and pacifism, Richard Evans has concluded that, during the first World War, 'feminist pacifism was the creed of a minority, of a tiny band of courageous and principled women on the far-left fringes of bourgeois liberal feminism'.[7] Bennett's fearlessness in stating her principles, however unpopular, emerges during this period, a characteristic that would be evident very much over the next forty years. That fearlessness extended to taking on James Connolly, not the last labour leader to be confronted by Bennett. During these years her sense of nationality was articulated, particularly through her key position in WILPF. To her, expression of nationality was in effect the ultimate human right. After the First World War, Bennett's disillusionment with the League of Nations is clear, as is her concern that 'The principle of nationality is essential to the security of all free peoples.'[8] While her persistent efforts to promote Irish independence in an international context were encouraged, her emphasis on internationalism was not always so welcome. During Bennett's illness in 1922, Rosamund Jacob informed Geneva that 'we simply cannot get our press to publish anything relating to internationalism'.[9] Even Jacob herself, on one occasion, wrote in exasperation that Bennett was 'too damn international in the anti-national sense'.[10] In the type of inward-looking society that developed in Ireland during the 1930s and 40s, such emphasis on internationalism continued to be viewed with suspicion.

Another significant influence on Bennett was the work of Sir Horace Plunkett and George Russell in the field of co-operative endeavour. Late in her life she recounted how she had in her youth regarded Plunkett's initiative with awe, and had been a regular visitor to Plunkett House to meet with Russell and Susan Mitchell. In particular Bennett had been greatly influenced by two books written by Russell, *Co-operation and Nationality* and *The National Being*.[11] Passages from the latter work clearly are reflected in Bennett's subsequent views on economic freedom for workers allied to the democratic control of industry, the effects of capitalism in limiting such development, a desire for more co-operative ventures and concern about the use of the strike as a weapon in economic warfare. Bennett supported the work of Muintir na Tire, hoping that through its work the aims of Plunkett could be attained. She also hoped that some day the Report of the Commission on Vocational Organisation would be taken down from its shelf in the Department of Industry, and looked at anew – despite its shortcomings – so that the integration of social elements for the common purpose of a co-operative commonwealth, such as Plunkett, Russell and Connolly had in mind, might be achieved.[12]

It is clear that a defining moment in Bennett's life came with her decision to work in the trade union movement. From the time of that commitment in 1916, her primary concern was for her members, 'her girls'. Over the coming decades, she would use every means at her disposal to improve their wages and working conditions. She visited their places of employment – factories, fruit farms, laundries and hospitals – to observe conditions herself. To ensure that she was in the strongest possible position when negotiating for her members, she consulted shop stewards regarding precise manufacturing requirements within specific industries. She urged women to form workers' councils and become involved within their firms. She sought to empower women workers through boosting their self-esteem, emphasizing their value within the workforce. Bennett was particularly insistent that IWWU staff take proper care of members' business, and would show her annoyance at any mistake or oversight.[13] One writer has noted that, 'Miss Bennett never saw the members of the Women Workers' Union as numbers in a register. They were always human beings entitled to a decent life.'[14] And she fought for that entitlement like a lioness, confronting employers fearlessly. Her members seem to have regarded her with a mixture of awe and affection. 'Miss Bennett', as she was popularly known, was an invaluable ally for women workers. Articulate, confident and, committed, she argued the women's cause with employers, uninhibited by class restraints.

Employers generally respected Bennett. In part this stemmed from the vigour with which she fought her case, allied to the fact that they felt that once she made a bargain, she would keep it. Her preference for conciliation rather than strike action no doubt added to this acceptance on their part. Yet Bennett's dominance as advocate for women workers, invaluable as it was, appears to have created something of a dependency syndrome within the union's membership. Factors contributing to this development would include the low self-image of women workers generally, and the reluctance of women to become active within the union. In addition, Bennett and her executive colleagues were significantly older than most of the membership. By staying in office well beyond normal retirement age, the executive officers did little to encourage a new generation of union leaders. For Bennett it seems that 'her girls' became the family she never had. In a press interview shortly after her retirement from the IWWU in 1955, Bennett referred to the fact that she had never married and had children of her own. She pointed out however that although she had officially retired from the union, 'I'll never be able to stop worrying about my thousands of children in it.'[15] Another press interview of the time described Bennett as 'the foster mother of thousands of Irishwomen'.[16] Bennett consistently sought to strengthen women's voice within the general trade union and labour movements. As outlined above, her persistent attempts to persuade the IWWU executive to become politically active were in the main rebuffed, with the Labour Party not providing any fundamental incentive.

Following a term as Vice-President of Congress in 1931, Bennett was elected as its first woman president in 1932. While this was in part due to her seniority within the trade union movement, it also confirmed acceptance of Bennett as a key public figure. With this achievement, Bennett broke the gender stereotype, and over the next two decades Helen Chenevix and Helena Molony of the IWWU would follow in her footsteps. Bennett herself served a second term as president in 1947–48. Following her first election as president in 1932, there recurred echoes of Sinn Féin criticism three years earlier, with some objection to a president being elected from outside the ranks of the working class. This criticism of Bennett was made from time to time during her career, and indeed on occasion since her death. Her middle-class background, elegant dress, confident manner and preference for settlement in dispute caused distrust in some quarters. No doubt the fact that she was female added to such distrust.

As has been noted, Bennett's public profile continued to rise between the 1920s and the 1940s. Arguments made by her in the public domain regarding key issues that emerged during those years have been detailed. But what of the private Louie Bennett? From the limited personal correspondence that has survived, we can glean a certain amount. While her early letters to both Sheehy Skeffingtons reflect current concerns with suffrage and pacifism, her later letters to Hanna reveal particular personal qualities. A practical nature, a belief in doing something concrete emerges. Writing to Hanna after her husband's murder, Bennett, while sympathetic and offering her help, suggests certain practical things that might be done to further the work and memory of Frank. Her letters to Hanna during her editorship of the *Irish Citizen* in 1920 reveal a keen business sense. Her correspondence with WILPF head office between 1915 and 1931 display a sharp mind, observant and critical, with a keen awareness of international affairs. All of these qualities were fused in her work within the trade union movement, fired by her goal to better the lot of the working woman. Diaries of contemporaries during the 1920s and 30s confirm these qualities, along with her single-mindedness and determination. The diversity of her activities is also revealed in these diaries. In 1921 Jacob refers to herself and Bennett standing outside Leinster House distributing leaflets regarding the Russian famine, while the following month she notes Bennett's attempts to get a press ticket to the Treaty debates in the Dáil. Jacob's 1935 diary reveals that Bennett had given her five shillings towards the Frank Edwards fund, approved the [Republican]Congress attitude, and was an admirer of Peadar O'Donnell and his books.[17] Dermot Keogh has noted that Bennett and Chenevix were among those who helped in the reception of refugees from mainland Europe during the late 1930s.[18]

Those who met Bennett through her public activities have recounted her strong personality and commitment to causes for which she campaigned. The late John Swift – who worked with her in the ITUC while wary of her vocational tendencies and her class background, acknowledged the sincerity of her commitment to women workers. Politically he considered her a moderate, with somewhat romantic ideals.[19] Referring to Bennett's tenure as president of the ITUC, Donal Nevin has described Bennett as a very firm woman, dogged in her point of view. He observed that Bennett was no wilting flower, 'she was a woman who'd push herself'.[20] The late Dr Noel Browne spoke of how much he cherished his friendship with Bennett, whom he described as an integral part of the protest movement. Noting that many of the women who got involved in political work or pressure groups ended up making the tea, Browne pointed out that there was no way anyone would *ever* have asked either Bennett or Chenevix to make tea.[21] Maura MacDonagh, who worked at one stage for Ruaidhri Roberts in Congress, described Bennett as a fantastic president of Congress, noting that 'no-one would write *her* speeches'.[22] The late Matt Merrigan referred to her militant attitude regarding women's rights, observing that

Bennett was a lion as far as employers were concerned.[23] John de Courcy Ireland has described her as hard but not harsh, very decisive in discussion, but always willing to listen to others. In addition to her concerns regarding poverty and housing problems in Dublin, de Courcy Ireland pointed to her interest in the concept of worker participation in the control of industry.[24]

Bennett's financial situation has been the source of some speculation. A belief that private means enabled her to work within the IWWU, added to her family background and upbringing, was a cause of criticism and resentment in some quarters. Bennett did inherit money after her mother's death in October 1929. Her share of this legacy amounted to approximately £2,300. She continued to live in Killiney, but moved into a newly built bungalow next door to Helen Chenevix's house, 'Tigeen'. Bennett later recalled with fond amusement that her mother had bought the house for her 'with the old fashioned idea that I, a poor defenceless female against the world, might have need of it. I remember how I laughed at her [at the time but] I've often remembered her thoughtfulness with gratitude .'[25] Bennett spent the remaining twenty-seven years of her life in this house – St Brigid's – looked after by her housekeeper Molly. While it would appear that she had a comfortable lifestyle, there are no indications of lavish or extravagant spending. Quite the contrary in fact. Her surviving papers indicate a modest and thrifty attitude towards financial matters, and at times hint at financial pressures. Although she was unmarried, Bennett had significant responsibilities. These included the care of her mother and her aunt during the 1920s and early 1930s, of her invalid brother, Lionel, during the 1930s and 40s, and provision for the education of her niece Mary. Her correspondence during these years reflected this thrifty outlook in her insistence on staying in modest accommodation when on trade union or WILPF business. Whether this was from necessity or choice is not clear. Mary Jones has noted that from 1920 all union officials were paid a salary, Bennett's salary being deemed appropriate to her position as General Secretary.[26] Referring to occasional complaints about rates of pay, Jones points out that the so-called 'big wages' paid to union officials were largely mythical. Following one such criticism in April 1920, Bennett offered to accept similar wages to a piece-worker, with the option of taking leave without pay if she so wished. Two years later, due to financial pressure within the union, Bennett and Molony accepted pay-cuts.[27] A former union employee recalled Bennett's view that trade union officials should be paid only one or two pounds more than workers.[28] Numerous references occur in her letters of the need to retain a salary. During her correspondence with WILPF head-office this issue emerges several times. In 1926 Bennett offered to organize WILPF's Dublin conference if they could pay her current salary of £20 per month for the period involved.[29] Again in 1930, she agreed to represent WILPF at a Women's Congress in India 'unfortunately, only on condition that all expenses are paid. I should have to surrender temporarily my post here, & I should still have to keep my house open & instal [sic] a friend in it to look after my aunt.'[30]

The issue of expenses for trips made to WILPF executive meetings occur regularly, and during 1932–33 there are clear indications that Bennett was having difficulty paying her subscriptions to the organization.[31] Following a trip to Geneva in April 1930, Bennett wrote to Sheepshanks, 'I am tired of being a wage slave! It deprives me of so many pleasant possibilities, and has driven me back to Dublin when I would so much rather be in Switzerland.'[32] IWWU records show a number of attempts by Bennett to resign from her position. Jones has argued that Bennett sometimes used the threat of resignation as a political ploy within the IWWU to establish her authority. While no doubt political manoeuvring occurred within the IWWU executive, what emerges clearly however is Bennett's wish to reduce her involvement in the day-to-day administration of the union, and have more time to concentrate on developing policy issues and research. Other factors contributing to this decision were recurring health problems (she had heart problems and diabetes) aggravated by an ever-increasing workload. When persuaded by the IWWU executive to abandon her retirement plans in 1930, Bennett requested that she be allowed to take extended leave of absence without pay from time to time, a deputy being appointed in her stead.[33] Provision for payment of the latter is probably why she sought reimbursement of her salary before taking on any project outside the union. It would appear that she felt she could cope during short periods without pay, and that perhaps she could earn from some free-lance journalistic work.

Another area of speculation has been the nature of the relationship between Bennett and Chenevix. That theirs was a close and lasting friendship based on common ideals is beyond doubt. From their initial involvement in the suffrage movement, both women shared a lifelong commitment to improving the lives of working women and to the causes of pacifism and non-militarism. From their first joint venture in the IWSF in 1911, they became almost like opposite sides of a coin. Family and friends all have testified to their quite differing personalities and appearances. Bennett was the more fiery, forceful, dominant personality, Chenevix more introverted, retiring, contemplative. In appearance they were equally distinct, Louie smartly dressed and groomed, Helen old-fashioned and plain by comparison. Yet no one who knew them personally or professionally underestimated either woman, both being seen as extremely capable, informed and intelligent. Chenevix was more of a loner than Bennett, not having a wide family circle.

In addition to strong family ties extending to a younger generation of nieces and nephews, Bennett had a wide range of friends within Ireland and abroad. Most, but not all of these, were women with similar interests and a background of active involvement in women's issues. In particular, Bennett was close to two other women, Ethel MacNaughton and Fanny Heron, both of whom she visited regularly. Among her other friends were Ronald J.P. Mortished, the writer Patricia Lynch and her husband R.M. Fox, Dr Theo Dillon and his daughter Marie Therese, and John de Courcy Ireland. Those personal letters of Bennett's which survive from the 1916–32 period and from 1950–1956, yield nothing regarding her feelings for Chenevix or her other friends. In contrast, her loving feelings towards her nieces and nephew come through very clearly. There were one or two occasions when Bennett discussed love and emotions. Writing to her niece Henrietta after the death of her father, Bennett noted 'It consoled me to think that Muriel [Louie's sister] has these happy memories of a love affair of such pure happiness. Theirs was a beautiful relationship.' In a surviving fragment of another letter, Bennett referred to an unidentified speaker whom she considered had placed too much emphasis on sex relationships, noting, 'Neither Muriel nor Helen nor I could remember in our childhood any particular feelings about the sex organs of little boys. We took the whole show for granted. Anyhow I can't help thinking that we might have a better world if less attention were given to sex relationships and more to personal relationships in other spheres.'[34]

Only a few of Chenevix's personal letters have come to light. In one, writing to a mutual friend the year following Bennett's death, she commented that, 'Louie Bennett was indeed a gallant soul, brimming over with courage and vitality.' She hoped that Fox's forthcoming biography would 'bring something of her inspiration to many people who hadn't the privilege of knowing her personally'.[35] In an appreciation of Bennett written for *The Irish Housewife*, Chenevix noted that Bennett 'had a personality unforgettable to all who knew her – full of vitality, gentle, yet fiery, daring and always lovable'.[36] Without any further letters or diaries it is impossible to define their relationship. It is clear that they were very close. They lived in neighbouring houses for some twenty-five years, and together for the last couple of years as Bennett's health failed.

In conversation with those who knew her, a number of key qualities recur. Bennett was fiery and passionate, and, while quick to lose her temper, was equally quick to forgive and forget. She never hesitated to take action when she felt it necessary, whether that meant putting pressure on government ministers, criticizing political and trade union leaders in the press or berating a man on Killiney beach for lashing a horse.[37] She was scrupulously honest, disliked deceit in any form, and had a strong puritan streak. Letters that have survived from her final years show the caring side of Bennett, compassionate, encouraging those who were down on their luck, supportive of family and friends at difficult times. Again her practical nature shows through with advice on health, career and relationships. Political topics inevitably occur in these letters. The range covered included Bennett's disenchantment with the Irish Labour Party, her worry over the atom bomb and, on one occasion, concern that a favoured niece planned to vote Conservative, Bennett noting 'I fear Churchill'. A somewhat mellowed Bennett emerges during these last five years, but still her indomitable personality shines through. She is not afraid to display her feelings. In the course of a letter to her niece, Henrietta, Bennett states, 'I have always loved my three nieces but you with a special love, like my love for John' (her nephew). On another occasion, she confides to Henrietta, 'I am so pleased to know you found me a satisfactory Aunt. But you sure did give me something to think about, when you passed the much-hated 16 year age.'[38]

Bennett had taken responsibility for the education of one of her nieces – Mary Manning – after her father's early death. Manning noted that Bennett was particularly pleased when Mary started a drama group within the IWWU. She also noted that Bennett could be quite tyrannical.[39] Her brother John recalled that his aunt was 'a very strong person, a remarkable woman'.[40] He was very close to his aunt, and described her quiet sense of humour, willingness to help anyone who was in trouble and her closeness to family at home and abroad. Another niece, Christabel, pointing to the private side of Bennett, recalled early memories of her Aunt Louie at family gatherings, sitting at the piano singing 'Sweet Alice Benbolt'. She also recounted that, during a year living abroad, she met her Aunt in Geneva. Having arranged to meet her at the railway station, Christabel – with the presumption of youth – expected that her elderly aunt would be anxious to go straight to her hotel and rest. Far from it! To her surprise, Bennett 's one desire was to have lunch out of doors with a glass of wine.[41] It is clear that the younger generation of her family were extremely fond of Louie. She did not lecture them, was very approachable and open in her outlook, and clearly enjoyed their company. Her letters show encouragement and support for her nieces in their marriages, one letter noting that 'we have drifted away from that old-fashioned conception of home [which is] more than ever of value in this modern age of hurry and noise and unhappy anxiety'. She elaborated that people like Henrietta and her husband could make their home a sort of haven for other people, wherein their friends could find refreshment of mind or spirit or material comfort for a couple of hours. Referring to a remark by her niece regarding her neglect of her friends, Bennett replied, 'Of course a wife must plan to make home pleasant for her husband, – but it's equally if not more important to make it a happy resort for the friends of both man and wife.'[42]

In the spring of 1950 Bennett offered her resignation from the post of General Secretary to the executive of the IWWU. By putting forward her resignation rather than her retirement, Jones argues that Bennett presented the executive with a dilemma, thereby emphasizing the fact that, 'A mutual and unproductive dependency between the General Secretary and her Executive had become apparent.'[43] This resulted in Bennett being persuaded to remain at her post – in one way or another – for another five years. Initially granted paid leave of absence for one year, she was later appointed Consultative Secretary, a position that continued up to 1955. As Jones points out however, her brief within the IWWU during this period did not change dramatically, and her authority and capacity for work continued unabated. Now in her eighties, Bennett's mind and grasp of current affairs was as sharp as ever. Health problems continued to be a cause for concern, and she was hospitalized for a time in 1954. Early in 1955, Bennett informed the IWWU executive that while she was willing to act as consultant if the need arose, 'the time has fully come for a pensionable position for me'. She assured them that her interest in the union would not be diminished in any way, 'even though I won't have the right to harangue you and argue with you'.[44] This time she did actually retire, her position being filled by Helen Chenevix. Describing her retirement as the end of an era in Irish trade unionism, the *Irish Times* noted that Bennett's drive and personality had become the union's motive force.[45] Bennett still wrote to the executive from time to time, and, while not 'haranguing' them, continued to make her views known about the direction to take. So, in April 1956, while congratulating the executive for its many successful enterprises, she regretted the continued lack of interest in world affairs, commenting that:

> It is extraordinary that Irish workers generally limit their attention to affairs within our own small island as if what happens in the big world outside us had no effect upon us and as if we had no responsibility regarding such happenings. The women of Ireland should step forward and arouse our stay-at-homes to look out on the world and consider what they can do to help forward this great job of world co-operation.[46]

Louie Bennett died at her home on Sunday 25 November 1956. She was almost eighty-seven years of age. The attendance at her funeral reflected the span of her life's work. Among those present were William Norton, Tánaiste and Minister for Industry and Commerce, along with politicians from both Dáil and Senate. A broad spectrum of trade unionism was present – including members of both congresses, and representatives of the Labour Court. Many individual employers with whom Bennett had worked attended, as did representatives of the Federated Union of Employers. Friends from the many groups and organizations with which she had been associated joined with Bennett's family and personal friends to say farewell. Shortly afterwards it was decided that a memorial be erected in her memory. A fund was established and it was decided that a seat be placed in her honour in Dublin's St Stephen's Green. It was felt that Bennett would have particularly liked this style of memorial, given her fondness for sitting out in her own garden. As with her funeral, contributors to the fund covered the broad canvas of Bennett's activities. Friends, family, colleagues and former adversaries were all represented there. Close to 150 individual and organizational contributions were received, as were donations from 25 trade unions. Among the eclectic list of contributors were Eamon de Valera and Samuel Beckett. The seat was unveiled on 25 September 1958 by Dublin's Lord Mayor, who, as Helen Chenevix observed, happened most appropriately to be a woman, Catherine Byrne. The seat was curved, in response to Bennett's frequent observation that traditional straight seats inhibited conversation.[47]

R.M. Fox's life of Louie Bennett was published in 1958. The book was widely reviewed, mostly favourably, some wishing it had been a more extensive work. An *Evening Mail* reviewer commented that the book made most interesting reading 'in spite of what some would consider an unpromising subject – the life of a woman trade unionist'.[48] In the *Irish Democrat* it was noted that Bennett was of the moderates because she believed in moderation, not because she was afraid of anybody, 'hence to conservatives she was a lioness, to the left a sympathetic, if sceptical, observer'.[49] Desmond Ryan commented in the *Irish Times* that Bennett could give hard knocks in the most graceful manner, and could write 'with a delicate acid geniality that spared neither friend nor foe nor herself'.[50] Another reviewer described Bennett as 'the constitutional counterbalance to Constance Markievicz',[51] while Terry Ward declared that, 'She must have been more than a middle class woman with a conscience. If that were all to it she would have found refuge in one of the many benevolent organizations of the period without embroiling herself in a militant trades union.'[52]

The reforms Bennett sought, whether social or political, were always constitutional. From a left-wing labour perspective, they were often deemed conservative. After her death, Sean O'Casey noted that Bennett had been an active and useful woman among women workers, but never a revolutionary, commenting, 'She was a trades unionist and contented to go no farther, which in its way was good, but left a lot undone'.[53] Joe Deasy, John Swift and Matt Merrigan have all referred to her political naïvety, particularly in regard to her admiration of Salazar and corporatism. Yet, even within the trade union movement, the term radical can be applied to Bennett. While her views regarding women's domestic role reflected accepted attitudes of her day, her wider demands for a role for women within trade unionism, allied to her consistent campaign for improved pay and conditions for working women, were seen as radical at the time. Her championing of the weakest economic groups of women workers was often challenged and resented by more powerful male-dominated unions, as well as by employers and politicians. On the broader canvas of female equality across all facets of society, her arguments were undoubtedly compromised by an ambiguous attitude towards married women working outside the home. Her personal preference for economic conditions in which the latter would not be necessary was allied to a pragmatic understanding of what the trade union movement and society in general would accept in this regard.

Bennett's initiation into public life through the suffrage campaign highlighted what would remain constant in her career, the attainment of reform through constitutional methods. Perhaps her most radical voice however, came through her pacifist conviction. From 1915, when she first spoke out clearly and defiantly against militarism in all its guises, to the last years of her life when she argued in support of Irish neutrality in a cold-war era, hers was a consistent voice against war and the armaments race. Allied to this was her ideal of internationalism, urging that Ireland should promote world peace and co-operation between nations, and not be intimidated by the great world powers. An understanding of her commitment to pacifism is vital in assessing her life's work. All issues were filtered through her pacifist consciousness. While she could be confrontational in pursuit of goals, her preference for negotiation and peaceful resolution determined her attitude to all forms of conflict – political or industrial. Her conciliatory attitude and lack of working-class credentials led to some criticism, yet she has been acclaimed by Ruaidhri Roberts as 'one of the most significant trade union leaders of the period'.[54] Perhaps best summed up by Desmond Ryan of the *Irish Times* as 'The Fighting Pacifist', Bennett was remembered by John Swift as one for whom democracy was measured, not by the privileges claimed by the majority, but by the rights assured to the minority. In 1911 Bennett had entered public life in the cause of women, and, to the end, she urged women to unite and become involved in all areas of public life. Some forty-four years later, on her retirement from the IWWU in 1955, Bennett saw dangers ahead for women, warning that, 'Despite the progress we have made, women still must unfortunately fight to hold their corner. They must organise with women all over the world. That is their weapon. That is their strength.'[55]

Notes and references

Abbreviations

American Commission, 1921	*Evidence on Conditions in Ireland Comprising The Complete Testimony, Affidavits & Exhibits presented before The American Commission* (Washington DC, 1921)
IWWUA	Irish Women Workers' Union Archive, Irish Labor History Museum, Dublin.
Jacob Diaries	Diaries of Rosamund Jacob, 1897–1960, NLI.
Kingston diaries	Diaries of Lucy O. Kingston, privately held
Minutes CVO	Minutes of Evidence, Commission on Vocational Organisation, which includes evidence of Joint Committee representing the National Council of Women of Ireland, the Joint Committee of Women's Societies and Social Workers, the Catholic Women's Federation of Secondary School Unions, NLI.
WILPF Colorado	Archives of the Women's International League for Peace and Freedom stored at Norlin Library, University of Colorado, Boulder, Western Historical Collection. Manuscripts referring to Ireland cited in this book are contained in Series 1, 11 and 111. For further details of this collection see Doris Mitterling and John A. Brennan, *A Guide to the Women's International League for Peace and Freedom Papers* (Norlin Library, University of Colorado, 1982).

1: The early years

1 Lady Henrietta Wilson to Rosemary Cullen Owens, October 1999.
2 R.M. Fox, *Louie Bennett, Her Life and Times* (Dublin, 1958).
3 Louie Bennett later recounted that her grandfather had remarried while on holiday with relatives in London. The first indication his family had of this event was a letter to his niece, advising of the date of his return, and

requesting that an extra pillow be put on his bed. Henrietta Wilson to author, October 1999.

4 Fox, *Louie Bennett*, p. 11.

5 Edward Dowden was Professor of English Literature and Oratory in Trinity College Dublin, 1867–1913. The first occupier of this Chair, he was a noted lecturer and expert on Shakespeare and Shelley. A strong Unionist, he was not an admirer of Irish literature or the Celtic revival. John Gwynn was Regius Professor of Divinity in Trinity College Dublin, 1888–1917. A learned scholar, both he and his son Edward (later Provost of TCD) became very interested in Irish and the Gaelic revival. I am indebted to Susan Parkes, Senior Lecturer in Education and Head of Department, TCD, for this information. See R.B. Mcdowell and D.A. Webb, *Trinity College, An Academic History* (Cambridge, 1982).

6 Fox, *Louie Bennett*, p. 13.

7 Ibid, pp. 11–12.

8 *American Commission*, 1921, p. 1046.

9 *Irish Times*, 7 February 1953.

10 Fox, *Louie Bennett*, p. 16.

11 Ibid, pp. 33–36.

12 Ibid, pp. 33–36.

13 Barry Pain to Louie Bennett, 12 October 1898, 20 June 1900 (papers in private hands); also Jack Louden, *O Rare Amanda, The Life of Amanda McKittrick Ros* (London, 1954), pp. 51–53.

14 Pain to Bennett, February–May 1901 (papers in private hands).

15 *American Commission*, 1921, p. 1047.

16 Louie Bennett, *A Prisoner of His Word* (Dublin, 1908), p. 148.

17 Fox, *Louie Bennett*, p. 16.

18 See Alan Hayes (ed.), *The Years Flew By, Recollections of Madame Sidney Gifford Czira* (Galway, 2000, revised 2nd edn).

2: Votes for women

1 For an in-depth study of the suffrage movement in Ireland, see Rosemary Cullen Owens, *Smashing Times, A History of the Irish Women's Suffrage Movement 1889–1922* (Dublin, 1984 and 1995).

2 *Irish Women's Suffrage and Local Government Association Annual Report* (Dublin, 1903), p. 7. [Hereagter *IWSLGA*].

3 J.J. and M.E. Cousins, *We Two Together* (Madras, India, 1950), p. 169.

4 *IWSLGA, Annual Report*, 1909, p. 20, and 1910, p. 21.

5 H. Chenevix, 'Louie Bennett' in *The Irish Housewife* (1959), p. 35.

6 *Irish Citizen,* 9 November 1912.

7 Cousins, *We Two Together,* p. 185.

8 Cullen Owens, *Smashing Times*, pp. 42–43.

9 *Irish Citizen,* 17 May 1913.

10 James Connolly, *The Re-Conquest of Ireland* (Dublin, 1917), p. 291.

11 Chenevix, 'Louie Bennett', p. 36.

12 *Irish Citizen,* 1 June 1912.
13 Ibid., 17 May 1913.
14 Ibid., 31 May 1913.
15 Ibid., 6 December 1913.
16 Ibid., 2 and 9 August 1913, 6 December 1913. For a more detailed examination of the interaction between labour and suffrage workers, see Rosemary Owens, 'Votes for Ladies, Votes for Women, Organised Labour and the Suffrage Movement, 1876–1922', in *Saothar* 9, 1983, pp. 32–47.
17 *Irish Citizen,* 17 October 1914.
18 Ibid., 17 May 1913.
19 Ibid.
20 Ibid., 9 October 1915.
21 Ibid., 17 October 1914.
22 Sheehy Skeffington Papers, National Library of Ireland, (hereafter SSP, NLI). MS 21194.
23 *Irish Citizen,* 8 June 1912.
24 Ibid., 27 July 1912.
25 Ibid., 5 July 1913.
26 Ibid., 17 May 1913.
27 *American Commission,* 1921, p. 1047.
28 *The Workers Republic,* 4 September 1915.
29 *To the Smaller Nations,* June 1919, Appeal from Irishwomen's International League, signed by Louie Bennett to WILPF, Geneva.
30 Fox, *Louie Bennett,* pp. 61–62.
31 Bennett to H. Sheehy Skeffington, 19 September 1916, SSP, NLI. MS 22,279 (5).
32 Bennett to H. Sheehy Skeffington, in folder May–September 1916, SSP, NLI. MS 22,279 (6).
33 D. Webb to H. Sheehy Skeffington, 3 July 1916, SSP, NLI. MS 22,279(3); also D. Webb to H. Sheehy Skeffington, 18 August 1916, SSP, NLI. MS 22,279 (4).
34 *Irish Citizen,* October 1917. (It was now published monthly).
35 Ibid., January 1920.
36 Bennett to Emily Balch, First International Secretary of WILPF, 11 March 1920 (WILPF Colorado).
37 Bennett to H. Sheehy Skeffington, 7 March 1920, SSP, NLI. MS 24,110.
38 Bennett to H. Sheehy Skeffington, 14 March 1920, SSP, NLI. MS 22,690 (3).
39 *Irish Citizen,* May–August 1920. (It was now published quarterly)
40 Ibid., 11 December 1915.
41 Ibid., January 1920.
42 Ibid., 7 February 1914.
43 Ibid., October 1919.
44 Bennett to H. Sheehy Skeffington, 30 July 1920, SSP, NLI. MS 24,112.

45 Marion Duggan to H. Sheehy Skeffington, 10 September 1920, SSP, NLI. MS 22,693 (5).
46 *Irish Citizen,* September–December 1920. The paper had recently become a quarterly.

3: Pacifism, militarism and republicanism

1 Richard Evans, *Comrades and Sisters: Feminism, Socialism and Pacifism in Europe 1870–1945* (Hemel Hemstead, 1987), chapter 5. See also Jill Liddington, *The Long Road to Greenham: Feminism and Anti-Militarism in Britain Since 1920* (London, 1989), pp. 37, 56, 58–59, 63.
2 Richard J. Evans, *The Feminists, Women's Emancipation Movements in Europe, America and Australia 1840–1920* [London 1977], pp. 251–252.
3 Among those in attendance were Charlotte Despard, Jane Addams, Charlotte Perkins Gilman, Kathleen Courtney, Helena Swanwick, Alice Parks and Mary Sheepshanks.
4 Margaret Mulvihill, *Charlotte Despard: a Biography* (London, 1989), p. 103.
5 *Jus Suffragii* (monthly journal of the IWSA), 1 December 1914, cited in Liddington, *The Long Road,* pp. 94–5. See also Anne Wiltsher, *Most Dangerous Women: Feminist Peace Campaigners of the Great War* (London and Boston, 1985), p. 57.
6 *Jus Sufragii,* 1 January 1915. The subtitle, *The International Woman Suffrage News,* was used from 1920, changing to *The International Women's News* in 1930; see also Rosemary Cullen Owens, 'Women and Pacifism in Ireland 1915–1932' in Maryann Valiulis and Mary O'Dowd (eds), *Women & Irish History* (Dublin, 1997).
7 Liddington, *The Long Road*; see also Adele Schreiber and Margaret Mathieson, *Journey Towards Freedom* (Copenhagen,1955). Addams was awarded the Nobel Peace Prize in 1931.
8 *Irish Women's Suffrage Federation Annual Report, 1913–14*; also minutes of IWSF executive 15 August 1914, 13 March 1915, SSP, NLI. MS 21,196.
9 *Irish Citizen,* 21 November 1914.
10 Bennett to Hanna Sheehy Skeffington, 1 October 1914, SSP, NLI. MS 22,667(2).
11 *Irish Citizen,* 11 December 1915.
12 Ibid., 11 December 1915.
13 Louie Bennett, 'Women of Europe, When Will Your Call Ring Out?' in *Jus Suffagii,* 1 March 1915.
14 Gertrude Bussey and Margaret Timms, *Pioneers for Peace, Women's International League for Peace and Freedom 1915–65* (London, 1965), p. 18; also Liddington, *The Long Road,* pp. 94–96.
15 Kingston diaries, March 1915.
16 Wiltshire, *Most Dangerous Women,* pp. 88–90; also Liddington, *The Long Road,* p. 105.
17 *Irish Citizen,* 24 April 1915. The delegates were Hanna Sheehy Skeffington,

Margaret McCourbrey and Mrs Metge from the IWFL, Louie Bennett. Miss Moser and Mrs Isabella Richardson from the recently formed Irish committee, and Helen MacNaghten from the Northern committee of the IWSF.

18 Evans, *Comrades and Sisters,* pp. 127–9. For an Australian perspective see Darryn Kruse and Charles Sowerwne, 'Feminism and Pacifism: "Woman's Sphere" in Peace and War' in *Australian Women, New Feminist Perspectives* (Melbourne, 1986).
19 *Irish Citizen,* 12 September 1914.
20 Ibid., 27 February 1915; for an examination of the conflicting positions of nationalist, unionist and pacifist feminists in Ireland see Dana Hearne 'The *Irish Citizen* 1914–1916: Nationalism, Feminism, and Militarism', in *Canadian Journal of Irish Studies,* 18, no. 1 (1992), pp. 1–14.
21 *Irish Citizen,* 22 May 1915.
22 Ibid.
23 Bennett to Hanna Sheehy Skeffington, 12 May 1915, SSP, NLI. MS 22,674.
24 Bennett to Hanna Sheehy Skeffington, 17 March 1915, SSP, NLI. MS 22,672.
25 Bennett to Hanna Sheehy Skeffington, 3 June 1915, SSP, NLI. MS 22,675.
26 *Irish Citizen,* 10 April 1915; for a study of the differing viewpoints of Bennett and Sheehy Skeffington, see Margaret Ward, 'Nationalism, Pacifism, Internationalism' in Anthony Bradley and Maryann Gialanella Valiulis (eds), *Gender and Sexuality in Modern Ireland* (Amherst, 1997).
27 *Irish Citizen,* 22 May 1915: published later in 1915 as a pamphlet.
28 Fox, *Louie Bennett,* Her Life and Times (Dublin, 1957), p. 48.
29 Helena M. Swanwick, *I Have Been Young* (London, 1935), pp. 281–282. Described by Liddington as 'a small Liberal intellectual elite', the UDC questioned Britain's involvement in the war, advocated the establishment of an international organization after the war to prevent other conflicts, and argued that peace terms should not be punitive. Among its founders were H.N. Brailsford, Bertrand Russell and Ramsay MacDonald. Liddington, *The Long Road,* pp. 81–83.
30 Bennett to Augustine Birrell, 19 April 1916, National Archives of Ireland, Chief Secretary's Office Registered Papers (1916), 7800.
31 *Irish Citizen,* 20 February 1915.
32 Bennett to Hon. Sec., ICWPP, 19 October 1915, 26 November 1915, 5 and 18 January 1916, 14 February 1916 (WILPF Colorado); also Bennett to Hanna Sheehy Skeffington, 19 June 1915, SSP, NLI. MS 22,648(11).
33 Bennett to Chrystal MacMillan, 5 January 1916 (WILPF Colorado).
34 Bennett to Chrystal MacMillan, 29 January 1916 (WILPF Colorado).
35 First yearly report of the Women's International League (WIL) October 1915 to October 1916. WILPF Papers, British Library of Political and Economic Science [Hereafter WILPF Papers BLPES].
36 *Irish Citizen,* October 1916.

37 Rosa Manus to Louie Bennett, 18 December 1916 (WILPF Colorado).
38 Minutes of Executive Committee, Irishwomen's Suffrage Federation, 30 June 1917, SSP, NLI. MS 21,196.
39 Bennett to Chrystal MacMillan, 15 January 1916 (WILPF Colorado).
40 Fox, *Louie Bennett,* p. 57.
41 Bennett to Hanna Sheehy Skeffington, (in folder marked May–September 1916), SSP, NLI. MS 22,279(6).
42 Letter from IIL to Messrs Lloyd George, Redmond and Dillon, 13 June 1916, sent to Rosa Manus, 12 July 1916 (WILPF Colorado).
43 IIL to ICWPP, January 1917 (WILPF Colorado).
44 Bennett to Rosa Manus, ICWPP, 8 May 1917.
45 This read: CONNRAD EADAR-NAISIUNTA BAN NA H-EIREANN.
46 'London Letter' in *Irish Citizen,* November 1918.
47 Mulvihill, *Charlotte Despard,* p. 132.
48 *Irish Citizen,* November 1918: also WIL - Special Executive Meeting 22 October 1918 (WILPF Papers BLPES).
49 Fox, *Louie Bennett,* p. 74.
50 Bennett to Dr Aletta Jacobs, 7 November 1918 (WILPF Colorado).
51 Hanna Sheehy Skeffington had also been chosen as a delegate but was refused a passport, *Irish Citizen,* June/July 1919.
52 This remains the name and headquarters of the organization. Proximity to the League of Nations offices was among the reasons for this location.
53 WILPF Colorado, May 1919.
54 Bennett, Hon. Sec. IIL, 'To the Smaller Nations', June 1919, (WILPF Colorado).
55 Bennett to Emily Greene Balch, 2 October 1920 (WILPF Colorado).
56 Ibid.
57 Evans, *The Feminists,* pp. 205–206, 233–234, 239; also Ellen Carol Du Bois, *Feminism and Suffrage, The Emergence of an Independent Women's Movement in America* (Cornell, 1978).
58 Bennett to Emily Balch, 13 April 1920 (WILPF Colorado).
59 Emily Balch to Bennett, 19 April 1920 (WILPF Colorado).
60 Minutes of Executive Committee, WIL 8 April 1921 (WILPF Papers BLPES).
61 Bennett to Emily Balch, 2 November 1919 (WILPF Colorado).
62 Bennett to Emily Balch, 1 January 1920 (WILPF Colorado).
63 Helena Swanwick, *I Have Been Young* (London, 1935), p. 336; also Minutes of Executive Committee and Report of WIL, October 1920 to January 1922 (WILPF Papers BLPES).
64 Jane Addams Memorial Collection, University of Illinois, Chicago. (I am indebted to Eibhlin Breathnach for this reference.)
65 *American Commission,* 1921, pp. 979, 998.
66 Ibid., p. 979.
67 Ibid., pp. 1002–3.

68 Ibid., p. 1002.
69 Ibid., p. 1046.
70 Ibid., p. 1036.
71 Ibid., p. 1042.
72 Ibid., pp. 1051–1052.
73 Charlotte H. Fallon, *Soul of Fire: A Biography of Mary MacSwiney* (Cork and Dublin, 1986), p. 68.
74 *Irish Women and the Irish Republican Army*, Broadsheet, NLI, ILB 300 p. 12 (item 94).
75 Bennett to Emily Balch, 21 March 1921 (WILPF Colorado).
76 R. Fanning, M. Kennedy, D. Keogh, E. O'Halpin (eds), *Documents on Irish Foreign Policy*, Vol. 1, 1912–1922 (Dublin, 1998), Document no.11, p. 17.
77 Fanning et al., *Documents on Irish Foreign Policy,* Document no. 103, p. 179.
78 Jacob diaries, 1922, NLI. MS 32, 582, no. 40.
79 Emily Balch to Bennett, 25 January 1922 (WILPF Colorado).
80 Bennett to Emily Balch, 30 January 1922 (WILPF Colorado).
81 Bennett, 'Notes on Passive-Resistance', March 1922 (WILPF Colorado).
82 Bennett to Sir James Craig 10 June 1922 (WILPF Colorado).
83 SSP, NLI. MS 21,194, no. 45; also Fox, *Louie Bennett,* pp. 76–79; A. Gaughan, *Thomas Johnson* (Dublin 1980), pp. 207–208.
84 Report by Marie Johnson to fourth Congress of WILPF, Washington, 1924 (WILPF Colorado).
85 Fox, *Louie Bennett,* p. 80.
86 Bennett to Emily Balch, 12 October 1922 (WILPF Colorado).
87 Kingston diaries, 1 December 1920.
88 Jacob diaries, 12 July 1922, NLI. MS 332,582, No. 41.
89 Bennett to Emily Balch, 12 October 1922 (WILPF Colorado).
90 Kingston diaries, 2 November 1922.
91 Ibid., 3 January 1923.
92 Annual Report of Irish Section, Women's International League 1922–23 (WILPF Colorado).
93 Ibid.
94 *Report of the Fourth Congress of the Women's International League for Peace and Freedom,* Washington, May 1924 (WILPF Colorado).
95 Bussey and Timms, *Pioneers for Peace,* p. 53.
96 Lucy Kingston to Madeleine Doty (International Secretary of WILPF 1925–27), 26 February 1926; Rosamund Jacob to Madeleine Doty, 23 March 1926 (WILPF Colorado); other committee members were Sybil Le Brocquy, Mrs M'Clintock Dix, Marie Johnson, Miss Molyneux, Miss Mills, Mrs J. Richardson, Miss M. Stephens, Miss G. Webb.
97 Lucy Kingston to Madeline Doty, 1 January 1926 (WILPF Colorado).
98 Bennett to Madeline Doty, 16 February 1926 (WILPF Colorado). Emphasis in the original.
99 Bennett to Madeline Doty, 3 April 1926 (WILPF Colorado).
100 Jacob diaries, 19 April 1926, NLI. MS 332,582, No. 52.
101 Bennett to Madeline Doty, 31 May 1926 (WILPF Colorado).

102 Fox, *Louie Bennett,* pp. 88–9.
103 Jacob diaries, 17 July 1926, NLI. MS 332,582, No. 53.
104 Report of the Fifth Congress of WILPF, Dublin, 8–15 July 1926 (WILPF Colorado).
105 Ibid., p. 63.
106 Jacob diaries, 12 July 1926, NLI. MS 332,582, No. 53.
107 Fox, *Louie Bennett,* p. 89.
108 Swanwick, *I Have Been Young,* pp. 450–452.
109 *The International Woman Suffrage News,* August–September 1926.
110 Kingston diaries, July 1926.
111 Bennett to Madeline Doty, 6 December 1926 and 19 December 1926 (WILPF Colorado).
112 Mary Sheepshanks (International Secretary of WILPF 1927–30) to Bennett, 20 November 1928 (WILPF Colorado).
113 Bennett to Mary Sheepshanks, 26 August 1928 (WILPF Colorado).
114 Bennett to Mary Sheepshanks, 22 July 1929 (WILPF Colorado).
115 Sinn Féin to WILPF, 25 October 1929 (WILPF Colorado).
116 Kingston diaries, 1 November 1929.
117 Bennett to Mary Sheepshanks, 30 November 1929 (WILPF Colorado).
118 Una M'Clintock Dix to Mary Sheepshanks, 1 February 1930 (WILPF Colorado).
119 Kingston diaries, 13 December 1929.
120 Una M'Clintock Dix to Mary Sheepshanks, 1 February 1930 (WILPF Colorado).
121 Bennett to Anne Zueblin (assistant to Mary Sheepshanks), 9 December 1930 (WILPF Colorado).
122 Rosamund Jacob to Camille Drevet (international secretary of WILPF 1930–34), 9 April 1931 (WILPF Colorado).
123 Evans, *Comrades and Sisters,* pp. 130, 150–151.
124 An Irish branch of the WILPF was reconstituted in 1991 in the wake of the Gulf War.

4: Trade unions and Irish women

1 Fox, *Louie Bennett,* p. 42.
2 *Irish Citizen,* 6 September 1913.
3 *The Workers' Republic,* 18 December 1915.
4 *Irish Citizen,* 2 August 1913.
5 Ibid., 7 February 1914.
6 Report of ITUC annual conference 1914, pp. 77–79.
7 Fox, *Louie Bennett,* p. 64; also C. Desmond Greaves, *The Life and Times of James Connolly* (London, 1976), p. 378.
8 Louie Bennett, 'With Irish Women Workers' in *The Irish Economist,* vols 7–8 (August 1922), pp. 294–301.
9 *American Commission,* 1921, p. 1001.

10 Fox, *Louie Bennett*, p. 49; also fragment of letter from Louie Bennett to Henrietta Wilson, 10 February (year not given, but c.1950).
11 Fox, *Louie Bennett*, pp. 45–50.
12 *American Commission*, 1921, p. 1004.
13 Fox, *Louie Bennett*, pp. 54–7.
14 *American Commission*, 1921, p. 1047.
15 Ruth Taillon, *When History was Made, The Women of 1916* (Belfast, 1996).
16 J. Anthony Gaughan, *Thomas Johnson* (Dublin, 1980), p. 74. William O'Brien, letter to the *Irish Times*, 2 May 1955.
17 Bennett, 'With Irish Women Workers', p. 295.
18 Profile of Bennett by Ann Daly in the *Irish Press*, 2 May 1955.
19 Bennett, 'With Irish Women Workers', pp. 295–6.
20 *Irish Citizen*, August 1917.
21 Bennett to Cecil Watson, Court Laundry, Dublin, 21 September 1917, (private collection of Robert Tweedy, former Manager of the Court Laundry).
22 Mary Jones, *These Obstreperous Lassies, A History of the Irish Women Workers' Union* (Dublin, 1988), p. 25.
23 Bennett, 'With Irish Women Workers', p. 298.
24 Louie Bennett, review of *Women in the Factory, An Administrative Adventure, 1893–1921* by Dame Adelaide Anderson, in *The Irish Economist*, January 1923, pp. 258–60.
25 Bennett, 'With Irish Women Workers', p. 297.
26 *Irish Times*, 28 February 1919.
27 *Irish Citizen*, 11 December 1915.
28 *Irish Citizen*, December 1916.
29 Ibid.
30 Ellen Hazelkorn, 'The Social and Political Views of Louie Bennett, 1870–1956' in *Saothar* 13 (1988), p. 36.
31 *Irish Citizen*, July 1917.
32 Ibid., November 1919.
33 Ibid., January 1920.
34 Ibid., December 1919.
35 Bennett, 'With Irish Women Workers', pp. 297–8.
36 Louie Bennett, 'Women and the Labour Movement' in *Dublin Labour Year Book* (Dublin, 1930) p. 40.
37 C. Cahalan, 'Women and the Irish Labour Movement' in ibid. (Dublin, 1930), p. 48.
38 Helena Molony, 'James Connolly and Women' in *ibid.*, p. 32.
39 *Irish Citizen*, November 1919.
40 Ibid., December 1918.
41 Arthur Mitchell, *Labour in Irish Politics 1890–1930* (Dublin, 1974), p. 98.
42 Michael Laffan, '"Labour must Wait": Ireland's conservative revolution'

in P. J. Corish (ed.), *Radicals, Rebels and Establishments, Historical Studies 15*, (Belfast, 1985), p. 215.

43 Louie Bennett, 'What the Workers can Do in the New Day' in W.G. Fitzgerald (ed.), *Voice of Ireland* (Dublin, 1924), p. 299.
44 *ITUC Report for 1918.*
45 *Irish Citizen*, February 1920.
46 Jones, *These Obstreperous Lassies*, p. 67.
47 Ibid., pp. 59–60; Bennett was President of the Labour Women's Council which worked with the Labour party.
48 Ibid., p. 60.
49 Mitchell, *Labour in Irish Politics*, pp. 162, 170.
50 Ibid., p. 278
51 Louie Bennett, 'What the Workers can do in the New Day', pp. 299–301.
52 Ibid.
53 Ibid.
54 Gaughan, *Thomas Johnson*, p. 186.
55 Mitchell, *Labour in Irish Politics*, p. 140.
56 Fox, *Louie Bennett*, p. 92. Between 1923 and 1929 Bennett contributed twelve articles to *The Irish Statesman* on issues including international co-operation and peace, the League of Nations, and women's unemployment.
57 J.J. Lee, *Ireland 1912–1985: Politics and Society* (Cambridge, 1989), pp. 124–127.
58 Mitchell, *Labour in Irish Politics*, p. 197; also Lee, *Ireland*, p. 127.
59 Jones, *These Obstreperous Lassies*, p. 87.
60 IWWU Executive Minutes 16 January 1930, quoted in Jones, *These Obstreperous Lassies*, p. 96.
61 Report of Irish Trade Union Congress (ITUC) Annual Meeting 1932.
62 Ibid.
63 Bennett, 'Women and the Labour Movement', p. 39.
64 Astrid McLaughlin, '"Received with politeness, treated with contempt". The story of women's protests in Ireland against the regressive implications of sections of the Conditions of Employment Act (1936) and Bunreacht na hEireann, The Irish Constitution of 1937' (unpublished M.A. thesis, University College Dublin, 1996).
65 Jones, *These Obstreperous Lassies*, p. 123.
66 *Irish Press*, 14 May 1935.
67 Cited in McLaughlin, 'Received with politeness', p. 21.
68 Irish Women Workers' Union, Seventeenth Annual Report (May 1935), p. 5.
69 Jones, *These Obstreperous Lassies*, p. 126.
70 ITUC, 41st Annual Report 1935.
71 *Irish Times*, 3 August 1935
72 ITUC, 41st Annual Report 1935.
73 Ibid.

74 Ibid.
75 *Irish Times,* 11 July 1935, cited in McLaughlin, 'Received with politeness', p. 26.
76 IWWU, Executive Minutes, 5 September 1935.
77 *Irish Times,* 21 November 1935; also *The Republican Congress,* 30 November 1935.
78 Margaret Ward, *Unmanageable Revolutionaries: Women and Irish Nationalism* (Dingle and London, 1983), p. 236.
79 Ibid., p. 237; also McLaughlin, 'Received with politeness', p. 52.
80 Mary Daly cited in Liam O'Dowd, 'Church, State and Women' in Chris Curtin, Pauline Jackson, Barbara O'Connor (eds), *Gender in Irish Society* (Galway, 1987), p. 27.
81 Ward, *Unmanageable Revolutionaries,* p. 239. For details of proposed articles relating to women see Ward, pp. 238–9; also McLoughlin, 'Received with politeness', p. 45.
82 *Irish Press,* 12 May 1937.
83 Louie Bennett, Private notes on proposed 1937 Constitution IWWUA.
84 Ibid.; also *Irish Press,* 15 May 1937.
85 Ward, *Unmanageable Revolutionaries,* p. 240.
86 IWWU Executive Statement, 7 June 1937, IWWU Archives.
87 *Irish Press,* 15 May 1937.
88 Ward, *Unmanageable Revolutionaries,* p. 239.
89 Bennett to Eamon de Valera, President of the Executive Council, 24 May 1937, Department of the Taoiseach, File S9880. National Archives of Ireland, Dublin.
90 IWWU, Annual Report 1937–38, p. 5; also Ward, *Unmanageable Revolutionaries,* p. 241.
91 Jacob diaries, 28 May 1937, NLI. MS 332,582, No. 81.
92 *Labour News,* 26 June 1937.
93 Ibid.
94 Ibid.
95 IWWU Executive Minutes, 8 July 1937.
96 Mary E. Daly, 'Women, Work and Trade Unionism' in Margaret MacCurtain and Donncha O'Corrain (eds), *Women in Irish Society: The Historical Dimension* (Dublin, 1978), pp. 71–81.
97 Louie Bennett, Presidential Address to Irish Trade Union Congress 1932.
98 Daly, 'Women, Work and Trade Unionism', pp. 76–77.
99 Ibid., p. 77.
100 Seamus Cody, John O'Dowd, Peter Rigney (eds), *The Parliament of Labour, 100 Years of the Dublin Council of Trade Unions* (Dublin, 1986), pp. 171–177.
101 *The Torch,* 5 July 1941.
102 Ibid., 26 July 1941.

103 Jones, *These Obstreperous Lassies,* p. 199.
104 R. Cullen Owens, conversation with R. Childers, 15 May 1990.
105 R. Cullen Owens, interview with Lady Wicklow (Eleanor Butler), May 1987.
106 *Irish Times,* 17 September 1945.
107 Ibid., 5 and 13 September 1945.
108 Mai Clifford, 'They gave us one week but we wanted two' in *Labour History News* (Autumn, 1986), p. 12.
109 Fox, *Louie Bennett,* pp. 67–68.

5: The later years

1 Joseph Lee, 'Aspects of Corporatist Thought in Ireland: The Commission on Vocational Organisation, 1939–43' in A. Cosgrave and D. McCartney (eds), *Studies in Irish History Presented to R. Dudley Edwards* (Dublin, 1979), pp. 324–346.
2 Louie Bennett to President de Valera, 4 January 1937, Department of the Taoiseach, file S9278, National Archives of Ireland.
3 Astrid McLaughlin, '"Received with politeness, treated with contempt". The story of women's protests in Ireland against the regressive implications of sections of the Conditions of Employment Act (1936) and Bunreacht na hEireann, The Irish Constitution of 1937' (unpublished M.A. thesis, University College Dublin, 1996), p. 42.
4 Jacob diaries, 25 February 1937, NLI. MS 32,582, No. 81.
5 *Irish Women Workers' Union, 22nd Annual Report 1938* (IWWU archives).
6 *Report of the Commission on Vocational Organisation* (Dublin, 1943), pp. 279–282, 414–417.
7 Minutes CVO, NLI. MS 930, vol. 9, pp. 3065–3080.
8 Ibid., p. 3076.
9 Ibid., p. 3077.
10 Ibid., pp. 3067–68.
11 Ibid., p. 3075.
12 Minutes CVO, evidence of Irish Women Workers' Union, NLI. MS 925, vol. 4, pp. 1309–1331.
13 Ibid., p. 1319.
14 Ibid., pp. 1318–1319.
15 Ibid., p. 1324; also evidence of National Union of Tailors and Garment Makers, MS 925, vol. 4, p. 1356.
16 Minutes CVO, evidence of Workers' Union of Ireland, NLI. MS 927, vol. 6, pp. 1773–1783.
17 CVO Report, Reservation No. 1 by Miss Bennett and Senator Campbell, 4 November 1943, pp. 477–480. Reservation published with CVO Report (Dublin, 1943).
18 Ibid.
19 Ibid.
20 *The Torch,* 9 September 1939, p. 2.

21 Ibid.
22 Louie Bennett in 'Farming Today', a supplement to the *Irish Times,* 23 February 1954.
23 Lee, 'Aspects of Corporatist Thought', pp. 333, 342.
24 Bennett to H. Sheehy Skeffington, SSP, NLI. MS 22, 693 (4).
25 Louie Bennett, 'The Order of Today – Build!' in *Dublin Magazine*, vol. 11, March 1925.
26 Mary Jones, *These Obstreperous Lassies, A History of the Irish Women Workers' Union* (Dublin, 1988) p. 152.
27 Minutes of Executive Committee of IWWU, 1 December 1938.
28 R. Collis, *To be a Pilgrim* (London, 1975) pp. 91–2.
29 Helen Chenevix, 'Louie Bennett' in *The Irish Housewife,* 1959 (annual publication).
30 Emmet O'Connor, *A Labour History of Ireland 1824–1860* (Dublin, 1992), p. 137.
31 Hilda Tweedy, *A Link in the Chain, The Story of the Irish Housewives Association 1942–1992* (Dublin, 1992), pp. 14–15.
32 Maura Laverty, 'Maids versus Mistresses' in *The Bell*, vol. V11, no. 1, October 1943, pp. 18–24.
33 Louie Bennett, 'The Domestic Problem' in *The Irish Housewife*, 1946 (1st in series of annual publications).
34 Minutes of Executive Committee IWWU, political wing, 3 October 1935.
35 Irish Women Workers' Union, annual report, 1937–38, p. 6.
36 Louie Bennett to Thomas Johnson, 5 February 1944, cited in J. Anthony Gaughan, *Thomas Johnson* (Dublin, 1980), pp. 378–379.
37 Louie Bennett, Presidential Address to Annual Congress of Irish Trade Union Congress 1948.
38 Dr C. McCarthy, 'The Development of Irish Trade Unions' in Donal Nevin (ed.), *Trade Unions and Change in Irish Society* in (Dublin, 1980), p. 29.
39 Louie Bennett to John de Courcy Ireland, 7 July 1946, John de Courcy Ireland Papers (University College Dublin Archives P29a/ 140 (I)).
40 Seamus Cody, John O'Dowd, Peter Rigney (eds), *The Parliament of Labour, 100 Years of the Dublin Council of Trade Unions* (Dublin, 1986), p. 190.
41 Ibid., p. 191.
42 Louie Bennett to Sean Lemass, Minister for Industry and Commerce, 24 October 1947 (IWWU archives).
43 Tweedy, *A Link in the Chain,* p.101.
44 Cited in Cody, O'Dowd, Rigney, *The Parliament of Labour*, p. 193.
45 Evanne Kilmurray, 'Joe Deasy: the Evolution of an Irish Marxist, 1941–1950' in *Saothar*, 13, 1988; also R. Cullen Owens, interview with Joe Deasy, 1989.
46 Jones, *These Obstreperous Lassies*, p. 219.
47 Minutes of Commission on Technical Education 1927, NLI. MS R39 (with thanks to Charlie Callan for this reference).

48 Ruaidhri Roberts, *The Story of the People's College* (Dublin, 1986).
49 Interview with Lady Eleanor Wicklow, May 1987.
50 Mary A. McNeill, *The Beginnings of the Irish Association for Cultural, Economic and Social Relations* (Belfast, 1982).
51 Interview with Lady Henrietta Wilson, August 1987.
52 Interview with Nell Allott, 1990.
53 Bennett to Seamus Scully, 9 August 1955 (in private hands).
54 Bennett to Mary O'Malley, 21 May 1952 (in private hands).
55 Bennett to Seamus Scully, 5 April 1955 (in private hands).
56 Bennett to Patricia Lynch, 9 April 1955 (in private hands).
57 Bennett to Mary O'Malley, 21 May 1952 (in private hands).
58 Mitchell, *Labour in Irish Politics*, p. 258; also Gaughan, *Thomas Johnson*, pp. 307, 310.
59 Bennett to Secretary, Dublin Trades Union Council, 11 December 1952 (IWWU archives).
60 Cited in Jones, *These Obstreperous Lassies*, p. 219.
61 Bennett to Mary O'Malley, 3 June 1955 (in private hands).
62 Bennett to Seamus Scully, 21 June 1955; Bennett to Mary O'Malley, 3 June 1955; Bennett to Professor J. Johnston, President, The Irish Association, 18 June 1955 (all in private hands).
63 Bennett to John de Courcy Ireland, 7 November 1953, UCD Archives, P29a /140 (5).
64 Bennett to Mary O'Malley, 3 June 1955 (in private hands).
65 Bennett to Seamus Scully, 21 June 1955 (in private hands).
66 Bennett correspondence to Mary O'Malley and Seamus Scully, 1952–56 (in private hands).
67 Bennett to Seamus Scully, 21 June 1955 (in private hands).
68 Louie Bennett, 'Motive in Industry' in *Ireland Today*, vol. 3, no. 1, January 1938, pp. 9–14.
69 Sean O'Faolain, 'Autoantiamericanism' in *The Bell*, vol. 17, no. 3, June 1951, pp. 57–59.
70 *The Bell*, April–June 1951
71 Bennett to Henrietta Wilson, 22 February 1950 (in private hands.)
72 Ibid.
73 Bennett to Henrietta Wilson, undated, but c.1950 (in private hands).
74 Bennett to Henrietta Wilson, 6 June 1956 (in private hands).

Conclusion

1 Interview with Christabel Childers, 18 November 1986.
2 Fox, *Louie Bennett*, pp. 17–18.
3 Interview with Mary Manning, June 1987.
4 Ethel Snowden, *The Feminist Movement* (London and Glasgow, undated but from content c.1918).
5 *Irish Citizen*, November 1919.
6 Karen Offen, 'Defining Feminism: A Comparative Historical Approach' in

Signs: Journal of Women in Culture and Society, vol. 14, no. 1, Autumn 1988, pp. 119–57.

7 Richard Evans, *Comrades and Sisters: Feminism, Socialism and Pacifism in Europe 1870–1945* (Hemel Hempstead, 1987), p.131.

8 Bennett, 'To the Smaller Nations', June 1919 (WILPF Colorado).

9 Rosamund Jacob to Emily Balch, 16 June 1922 (WILPF Colorado).

10 Jacob diaries, 28 June 1925, NLI. MS. 32,582, No. 50.

11 George Russell, *Co-Operation and Nationality* (Dublin, 1912, republished 1982); George Russell, *The National Being,* (Dublin, 1916, republished 1982).

12 Bennett in 'Farming Today', a supplement to the *Irish Times,* 23 February 1954.

13 Interview with June Winders, November 1986.

14 G. Sweeney, 'Women in the Irish Labour Movement, Part 1', in *The Civil Service Review,* vol. 32, no. 3, July–August 1975, pp. 15–17.

15 *Irish Press,* 2 May 1955.

16 *Reynolds News,* series of interviews by Sheila Greene, undated but early 1950s (IWWU archive).

17 Jacob diaries, 20 February 1935, NLI. MS 32,582, No. 77. Edwards had been dismissed from his teaching post in Waterford following his attendance at the anti-fascist Republican Congress Convention of 1934 in defiance of his bishop.

18 Dermot Keogh, *Jews in Twentieth-Century Ireland* (Cork, 1998), p. 138.

19 Interview with John Swift, December 1986.

20 Interview with Donal Nevin, February 1991.

21 Conversation with Dr Noel Browne, 6 April 1987.

22 Interview with Maura MacDonagh, July 1990.

23 Interview with Matt Merrigan, August 1999.

24 Interview with John de Courcy Ireland, March 1991.

25 *Irish Press,* 2 May 1955.

26 Mary Jones, *These Obstreperous Lassies, A History of the Irish Women Workers' Union* (Dublin, 1988), p.48.

27 Ibid., pp. 48, 61–62.

28 Interview with Mary Martin, November 1986.

29 Bennett to Madeleine Doty, 9 March 1926 (WILPF Colorado).

30 Bennett to M. Sheepshanks, 30 November 1930 (WILPF Colorado). This trip did not take place.

31 Bennett to Camille Drevet, 12 September 1932 and 22 May 1933 (WILPF Colorado).

32 Bennett to Mary Sheepshanks, 28 April 1930 (WILPF Colorado).

33 Bennett to the President, Irish Women Workers' Union, 30 October 1930. IWWUA.

34 Bennett to Henrietta Wilson, undated fragment of letter, 1950–56 (in private hands).

35 Helen Chenevix to Seamus Scully, 3 October 1957 (in private hands).

36 Helen Chenevix, 'Louie Bennett' in *The Irish Housewife,* 1959 (annual publication).
37 Interview with Henrietta Wilson, August 1987.
38 Bennett to Henrietta Wilson, undated, but probably July 1955 (in private hands).
39 Interview with Mary Manning, 1987.
40 Interview with John Manning, October 1986.
41 Interview with Christabel Childers, 18 November 1986.
42 Bennett to Henrietta Wilson, undated, but probably spring 1955 (in private hands).
43 Jones, *These Obstreperous Lassies*, p. 203.
44 Bennett to IWWU Chairman, 6 January 1955. IWWUA.
45 *Irish Times*, 29 April 1955.
46 Bennett to IWWU, 30 April 1956 . IWWUA.
47 *The Evening Mail*, 25 September 1958.
48 *The Evening Mail*, 20 March 1958.
49 *The Irish Democrat*, July 1958.
50 *Irish Times,* 3 May 1958. Thirty years after her death Bennett was remembered by the Labour Women's National Council, who quoted her in their card for International Women's Day, 8 March 1986. Two years later that same group laid red roses on her seat in St Stephens Green. In 1996, Bennett was commemorated by a postage stamp in the 'Europa' series on famous women.
51 *Irish Times,* 5 March 1958.
52 Copy of newspaper review by Terry Ward 5 March 1958 in IWWUA. (title missing).
53 Sean O'Casey to Seamus Scully, 4 February 1957, cited in David Krause, *The Letters of Sean O'Casey*, vol. 3 (Washington DC, 1989), p. 381.
54 Ellen Hazelkorn, 'The Social and Political Views of Louie Bennett 1870–1956' in *Saothar* 13 (1988), pp. 32–44.
55 *Irish Press,* 2 May 1955.

Guide to further reading

Sources for further information on the life of Louie Bennett are unfortunately quite scarce. The only biographical work to date is that of R.M. Fox, published in Dublin in 1958. Based on a series of interviews with Bennett during the last year of her life, Fox's book, *Louie Bennett, Her Life and Times,* depends heavily on Bennett's memories of events during her life. At a time when many of Bennett's associates would have been alive, and when it might have been more feasible to obtain access to contemporary papers, it is unfortunate that Fox did not research his subject matter in more depth.

References to Bennett occur in more recently published material, most notably in Mary Jones, *These Obstreperous Lassies: A History of the Irish Women Workers' Union* (Dublin, 1988). In addition, *Saothar: Journal of the Irish Labour History Society,* 13, (1988), contains an article by Ellen Hazelkorn on 'The Social and Political Views of Louie Bennett, 1870–1956'. Jones' work covering the history of the IWWU from 1911 to 1984, is quite negative regarding Bennett. Hazelkorn, while also critical, attempts to be more comprehensive regarding the totality of Bennett's career.

A major problem regarding research on Louie Bennett has been the absence of any large volume of personal papers. Information on her early life has been based on her personal reminiscences to Fox, and on family recollections and anecdotal information. Her public career within the suffrage and trade union movements has been accessed mainly through the Sheehy Skeffington papers in the National Library of Ireland, and through records of the IWWU. The records of the

Women's International League for Peace and Freedom, at the University of Colorado, has yielded much valuable information on her pacifist involvement. Personal papers held in private hands, referring to the last decade of Bennett's life, have provided a key insight into her actions and concerns.

Index